10

MINUTE GUIDE TO

NETSCAPE™
FOR
WINDOWS® 95

by Galen A. Grimes

A Division of Macmillan Computer Publishing
201 West 103rd St., Indianapolis, Indiana 46290 USA

International Standard Book Number: 0-7897-0570-2
Library of Congress Catalog Card Number: 95-70638

97 96 95   3 2 1

Interpretation of the printing code: the rightmost number of the first series of numbers is the year of the book's printing; the rightmost number of the second series of numbers is the number of the book's printing. For example, a printing code of 95-1 shows that the first printing of the book occurred in 1995.

President and Publishert Roland Elgey

Publisher, Que New Technologies Stacy Hiquet

Publishing Director Brad R. Koch

Editorial Services Director Elizabeth Keaffaber

Managing Editor Sandy Doell

Director of Marketing Lynn E. Zingraf

Senior Series Editor Chris Nelson

Publishing Manager Tom Bennett

Acquisitions Editor Beverly M. Eppink

Product Director Mark Cierzniak

Production Editor Noelle Gasco

Copy Editor Dianna Evans

Technical Editors Alfonso Hermida, Don Doherty

Technical Specialist Cari Ohm

Operations Coordinator Patricia J. Brooks

Editorial Assistant Andrea Duvall

Acquisitions Coordinator Ruth Slates

Book Designer Kim Scott

Cover Designer Dan Armstrong

Production Team Lisa Daugherty, Chad Dressler, DiMonique Ford, Amy Gornik, Carla Hall, Damon Jordan, Bob LaRoche, Stephanie Mineart, Kaylene Riemen, Michael Thomas, Karen York

Indexers Brad Herriman, Kathie Venable

To Barb and JB, thanks. You both helped make this book possible.

ABOUT THE AUTHOR

Galen Grimes lives in a quiet, heavily wooded section of Monroeville, Pennsylvania, a suburb of Pittsburgh, with his wife Joanne and an assortment of deer, raccoons, squirrels, possums, and birds, which are all fed from their backdoor. Galen is also the author of several other Macmillan Computer Publishing books, including Sam's *First Book of DR DOS 6*, and Alpha's *10 Minute Guide to NetWare, 10 Minute Guide to Lotus Improv*, and *Windows 3.1 HyperGuide*. Galen has a masters degree in Information Science from the University of Pittsburgh, and by trade, is a project manager and NetWare LAN administrator for a large international bank and financial institution.

ACKNOWLEDGMENTS

Special thanks to our book-building team: Beverly Eppink, Mark Cierzniak, Noelle Gasco, Andrea Duvall, Alfonso Hermida, Don Doherty, and all the folks in Proofreading and Layout. None of this would have been possible without your long hours and patience with me.

CONTENTS

Introduction

Much of the mystery of the Internet has been lifted during the past few years. Getting on the Internet now is almost as easy as dialing a telephone—a far cry from the days of using arcane UNIX shell commands at a text-only terminal. Not only is the Internet much easier to access and use, once you get there, you'll see that there's more to see and do. With the introduction of the World Wide Web a few years ago and the release of Web browsing tools, like the original Mosaic, the Internet is a lot busier than it used to be.

Netscape, a second-generation Web browsing tool, has helped to bring even more people onto the Internet. Its ease of use and improved performance have made Web browsing easier, quicker, and a lot more fun.

Welcome to the *10 Minute Guide to Netscape for Windows 95*!

Netscape is not a particularly difficult program to use. Most Web browsers aren't. But knowing how to use most of its major features will make using it easier. That's where the *10 Minute Guide to Netscape for Windows* comes in. In just a few short lessons, you will have a better sense of what you can do with Netscape, and how to use it to make not only Web browsing easier, but also FTP downloads, sending e-mail, and browsing newsgroups.

How To Use This Book

The first few lessons in this book merely serve to get you through the basics of using Netscape. From there, you need read only the lessons that directly pertain to how you use the Internet. If you download files from FTP servers, then by all means take a look at the lessons on accessing FTP servers. The same goes for using Gopher servers to locate detailed information on particular topics, or using newsgroups.

CONVENTIONS USED IN THIS BOOK

You'll find icons throughout this book to help you save time and learn important information fast:

 Timesaver Tips   These give you insider hints for using Netscape more efficiently.

 Plain English   These icons call your attention to definitions of new terms.

 Panic Button   Look to these icons for warnings and cautions about potential problem areas.

You'll also find common conventions for steps you will perform:

What you type	Things you type will appear in bold, color type.
Press Enter	Any keys you press or items you select with your mouse will appear in color type.
On-screen text	Any on-screen messages you will see will appear in bold type.
New terms	New terms will appear in italic.
Press Alt+F1	Any key combinations you press will appear in this format.

TRADEMARKS

All terms mentioned in this book that are known to be trademarks have been appropriately capitalized. Que Corporation cannot attest to the accuracy of this information. Use of a term in this book should not be regarded as affecting the validity of any trademark or service mark.

Windows is a registered trademark of Microsoft Corporation.

Netscape, Netscape Communications, Netscape Navigator, and the Netscape Communications logo are trademarks of Netscape Communications Corporation.

Screen reproductions in this book were created by means of the program Collage Plus from Inner Media, Inc., Hollis, NH.

STARTING AND EXITING NETSCAPE

In this lesson, you learn how to start and exit Netscape. You also learn about the Netscape screen and home page, and how to get help online.

Home Page   A home page is merely the name given to the beginning screen or first page of a Web site belonging to a company, group, or organization on the World Wide Web. You could say it is analogous to a welcome screen. Occasionally, you will also see home pages by individuals.

STARTING NETSCAPE

Netscape is a Windows application, which means you have to be running Windows to run Netscape.

Running Windows!   Running Windows can be accomplished in several ways, and each will allow you to also run Netscape. You can run Windows as Windows 95, Windows NT, or one of the earlier versions of Windows, Windows 3.1 or Windows for Workgroups. Windows also runs under IBM's OS/2 Warp. In this book, however, running Windows means running Windows 95.

Once Windows is running, you can start Netscape. Here's how:

1. Click the Start button on the taskbar to open the Start menu. Choose Programs to open the Programs menu. Choose Netscape to open the Netscape menu (see Figure 1.1). Choose Netscape to start Netscape.

FIGURE 1.1   Starting Netscape.

 Where's the Icon? If you can't find the Netscape menu option, there's a good chance you haven't installed the program yet. Check the appendixes for instructions on downloading and installing the program.

2. The program starts and displays Netscape's home page (see Figure 1.2). If this is the first time you've started Netscape, you will see the license agreement before the home page.

 Where's Netscape's Home Page? If you start Netscape and the Netscape home page is not displayed, it is possible that your connection to the Internet has either been broken or is not set up correctly. If necessary, check with your Internet provider to make sure you are properly connected.

Directory buttons
locate other computers
and Web pages

Security colorbars

The toolbar displays
Displays the location   Netscape's commonly   The "N" icon pulses
of the Web page   used commands   to indicate activity

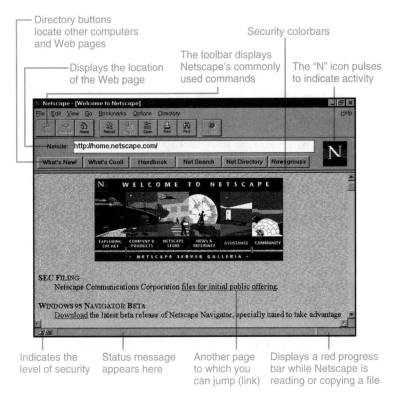

Indicates the   Status message   Another page   Displays a red progress
level of security   appears here   to which you   bar while Netscape is
   can jump (link)   reading or copying a file

FIGURE 1.2 Netscape's home page.

UNDERSTANDING NETSCAPE SCREEN PARTS

Besides the usual Windows screen features—title bar, minimize/
maximize buttons, windows borders, and so on—Netscape has
its own unique set of screen features. Figure 1.2 shows these
unique features:

- **Location field**   displays the location of the Web page you are viewing, or the name of the computer on which it is running, and the name of the file.

- **Status indicator**   the "N" icon pulses to indicate some level of activity in the background (such as copying a picture that is part of the current screen, copying additional text that isn't appearing on your screen yet, etc.), usually while you are moving to a new page or while part of the current page is being read by your computer.

- **Progress bar**   displays a red bar to indicate the progress of Netscape while reading the current page or copying a file to your computer (downloading).

- **Toolbar**   displays Netscape's most commonly used commands as icons.

- **Directory buttons**   these are preset to other pages on the World Wide Web, which you can use to locate other computers and Web pages.

- **Security indicator**   indicates whether the current page is set to a certain level of security; a solid, highlighted key indicates a high level of security; a broken key indicates low or no security.

- **Status message**   shows messages of importance to you from Netscape; these are usually links to other pages or computers.

- **Link**   another page to which you can jump; it is usually indicated by a different color and/or underlined text.

- **Security colorbars**   another type of security indicator; blue bars indicate a secure page, gray bars indicate it's not secure; most of the bars you will see will be gray.

GETTING HELP ONLINE

Help for Netscape is only available online. As with other Windows programs, help is available through the Help menu (see Figure 1.3).

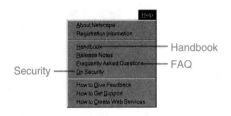

FIGURE 1.3   Netscape's Help menu.

Netscape provides a lot of information on its Help menu in addition to help. There are listings on registration, release notes, and security.

Help is found under three listings:

- Handbook
- Frequently Asked Questions
- On Security

Of these three, you will likely find the most useful information under **Handbook** and **Frequently Asked Questions**, also known as FAQs.

EXITING NETSCAPE

To exit Netscape, open the File menu and choose Close or Exit. Alternatively, you can simply press Ctrl+W.

In this lesson, you learned how to start and exit Netscape, and about the parts of its screen. In the next lesson, you learn how to use Netscape's toolbar to navigate through the Web.

NAVIGATING AND JUMPING TO YOUR FIRST WEB SITE

In this lesson, you learn about Netscape's toolbar and how to use the four navigational icons.

WHAT IS THE TOOLBAR?

Netscape's toolbar is a set of icons that you can use to quickly execute the most commonly used commands in Netscape. For example, anytime you want to return to Netscape's home page, you can click the icon labeled Home and the Netscape home page will reappear.

The toolbar is located near the top of the Netscape screen. The nine Netscape toolbar icons follow, along with a brief explanation of what each one does.

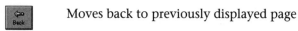	Moves back to previously displayed page
	Moves forward to previously displayed page
	Displays the home page
	Reloads an image being downloaded
	Displays images onto current page if they were not loaded automatically

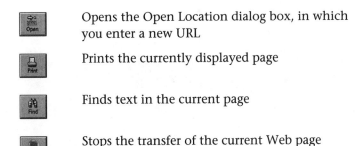

Opens the Open Location dialog box, in which you enter a new URL

Prints the currently displayed page

Finds text in the current page

Stops the transfer of the current Web page

Let's take a closer look now at how the navigational icons in the toolbar work. For reasons you'll understand later, we will not proceed in the order in which the icons are set.

USING OPEN TO JUMP TO WEB SITES

The Open icon is used to jump to a new site on the World Wide Web (from now on, it will be referred to simply as the Web):

1. Open the File menu and choose Open Location, or click the Open icon. The Open Location dialog box appears (see Figure 2.1).

FIGURE 2.1   The Open Location dialog box.

2. Type the following URL to go to the home page of the White House:

   http://www.whitehouse.gov

URL   URL stands for Uniform Resource Locators, which are the standard addresses indicating how to find a page or resource on the Web or the Internet, regardless of whether it is on a computer in the next state or two continents away.

3. Click the Open button, or press Enter. In a few seconds, the home page of the White House appears on your screen (see Figure 2.2).

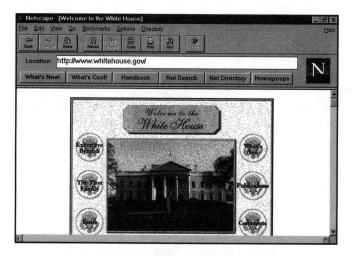

FIGURE 2.2   The White House home page.

The White House Did Not Appear!   URLs are *case-sensitive*, so make sure you typed it exactly as it is shown and be sure to include forward slashes (//), not back-slashes (\\).

If you're still having trouble reaching the White House, keep in mind that the "visitor" limit might have been reached. Web sites do have limits (different for each site), and busy sites reach their limit often.

NAVIGATING WITH BACK AND FORWARD

The Back and Forward icons are used primarily as navigational tools after you have viewed a series of pages. The Back icon is used to return you to the page you were on previously. The Forward icon is used to take you forward one page. Obviously, you can't go back or forward until you have viewed several pages. So, let's go to the Guest Book page:

1. Use the vertical scroll bar, located on the right side of the screen, to scroll down to just below the picture of the White House and click the Guest Book icon. This takes you to the Guest Book page (see Figure 2.3).

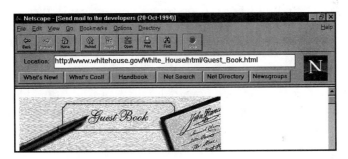

FIGURE 2.3 The Guest Book page.

2. Click the Back icon and you return to the White House home page.

3. Now click the Forward icon to go back to the Guest Book page. If you'd like, scroll down and sign your name in the guest book and leave a message for Bill and Hillary.

TIP **Quickly Going Back or Forward** A quick way to move back or forward through Web pages is to use your right mouse button. On the current Web page, click your right mouse button to open a small dialog box. Select Back to go back to the previous page. Select Forward to go forward.

RETURNING HOME

The Home icon is used to return to Netscape's home page:

1. Click the Home icon to return to Netscape's home page.

2. Click the Open button and try visiting a few new Web sites listed on the inside front and back covers. This will also give you some practice using the Forward and Back icons.

In this lesson, you learned how to use the four navigational icons in Netscape. In the next lesson, you learn how to use the remaining toolbar icons.

USING THE NON-NAVIGATIONAL ICONS

In this lesson, you learn about Netscape's "non-navigational" icons.

NETSCAPE'S NON-NAVIGATIONAL ICONS

In Lesson 2, you were introduced to the icons on Netscape's toolbar, especially the icons used to navigate the Web. In this lesson, you learn about the "non-navigational" icons Stop, Reload, Print, and Find.

STOPPING AND RELOADING FILES

You've probably noticed that each time you jump to a new Web page, it takes several seconds for all of the graphics and text to download so they can be displayed on your screen. If the page has a large graphic or numerous small graphics, these several seconds can easily become several minutes, especially if you have a slower modem. Sometimes, you might not want to wait for all of the graphics to download, especially if you are visiting a Web page you've visited before. The Stop icon allows you to stop downloading the graphic files and just display the text contained on the page. You learn how to view specific files in later lessons.

Download   Download simply means to copy a file from another computer to yours. When you jump to a new Web page in Netscape, it will automatically download the text and graphic files in that page to your computer so they can be displayed.

When a graphic file is downloading, you'll see its progress at the bottom of the screen:

Document Received *xxxx* of *xxxx* bytes.

Graphic Files   The files you see on the Web are 1) text files, which are letters and words, and 2) graphic files, which are pictures or images.

The first number will increment as more of the file is received. The second number shows the size of the file you are downloading.

The Reload icon is used to reload a Web page that you stopped or that, for some reason, did not fully load.

Here's how to use the Stop and Reload icons:

1. Open the File menu and choose Open Location, or click the Open icon. In the Open Location dialog box, enter the following URL:

    http://www.cmu.edu

2. While the counter is incrementing, click the Stop icon to stop downloading the current file. Your screen should look similar to Figure 3.1.

3. Now click the Reload icon to reload the stopped page. When the full page has completed downloading, you see the home page shown in Figure 3.2, which is the home page of Carnegie Mellon University, in Pittsburgh.

FIGURE 3.1   Using the Stop icon to stop a file download.

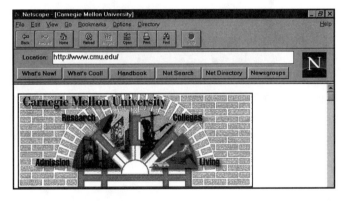

FIGURE 3.2   The CMU home page.

IMAGES

The Images button is one that you will rarely, if ever, have to use. It is designed to load images (pictures or graphics) onto the screen. In most cases, Netscape does this automatically. By default, when you install Netscape, the Options, Auto Load Images menu item is selected. If you deselect this menu item, you may have to use the Images button to load images if they are represented by icons.

LOCATING TEXT WITH FIND

The Find icon is used to locate text—either words or phrases—within the currently displayed Web page. Here's how it works:

1. Open the File menu and choose Open Location, or click the Open icon. In the Open Location dialog box, type:

   http://www.mit.edu

   This takes you to the home page of the Massachusetts Institute of Technology.

2. Click the Find icon to display the Find dialog box, as shown in Figure 3.3.

FIGURE 3.3   The Find dialog box.

3. Type the letters **mit** and click Find Next. The search finds the first instance of the letters **mit**.

4. Continue clicking Find Next to find all 16 instances of the letters **mit**.

Clicking Find Next will continue the search until all instances of the designated text are found. When you see **Search String Not Found!**, it means that all instances of the designated text have been found. You'll also notice that you can search forward or backward at any point in the page by selecting the Up or Down radio buttons in the Direction area of the Find dialog box. You can also select the Match Case check box if you are looking for an exact match.

PRINTING WEB PAGES

The Print icon does just what you would expect; it prints the current page, just as you see it on the screen. To print the MIT home page, select the Print icon. In a few seconds, the MIT home page will be reproduced on your printer.

In this lesson, you learned how to use the remaining toolbar icons. In the next lesson, you will learn about "links" and how to move through a Web page.

USING LINKS TO NAVIGATE A WEB PAGE

In this lesson, you learn about links and how to move through Web pages.

WHAT ARE LINKS?

If you haven't discovered by now from the few Web pages you've visited, pages are not merely isolated locations on the World Wide Web. The vast majority of pages you'll see contain connections to other Web pages. These connections are called *links*.

 Links Links are just what you think they are—they connect text or pictures from one page to another page. Links that are text—that is, letters and words—are usually shown as a different color and/or are underlined in a Web page. The mouse cursor changes from an arrow to a hand when placed over a link.

Links are based on the concept of *hypertext*.

 Hypertext Hypertext is text that contains links. These links provide additional information about certain keywords or phrases.

HOW TO IDENTIFY LINKS

When using Netscape, most Web page links are easy to identify. Let's go to a Web page with a lot of links. Click the Open button. In the Open Location dialog box, type:

http://cirrus.sprl.umich.edu/wxnet/

This is WeatherNet (see Figure 4.1).

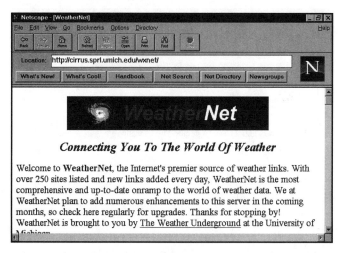

FIGURE 4.1   WeatherNet, courtesy of The Weather Underground.

As you scroll down through the first few paragraphs, notice that some of the words and phrases are underlined. If you position the cursor on the underlined text (see Figure 4.2), Netscape displays the name of a new Web site in the status message line. This is a link.

My Page or Links Are Not the Same!   Don't panic if this page or any other page shown in this book is different from what you see when you're browsing the Web. Web pages are constantly changing. Occasionally, they even disappear. This is a normal part of the dynamic nature of the Web.

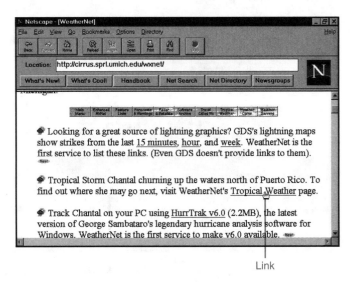

Link

FIGURE 4.2   Hypertext link on a Web page.

Scroll down to the section titled Servers and click the link EarthWatch Communications to go to the EarthWatch Communications home page (see Figure 4.3).

Scroll down to where you see Satellite Imagery and click either the text link or the satellite image of North America (see Figure 4.4).

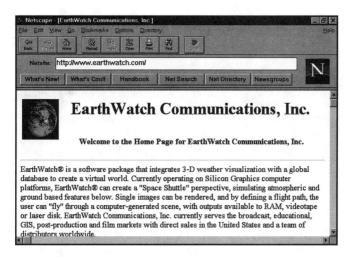

FIGURE 4.3   EarthWatch Communications' home page.

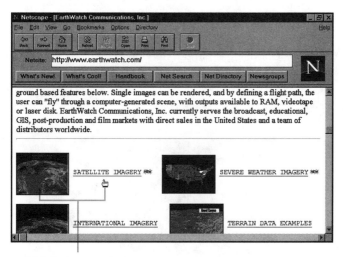

Click the image or text

FIGURE 4.4   Satellite weather imagery on the EarthWatch
Communications Web server.

On the next page, click where it says **Click HERE to see a 3-D perspective of cloud imagery over the eastern United States** (see Figure 4.5).

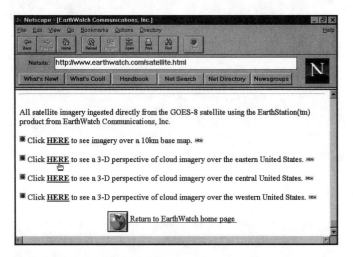

FIGURE 4.5   Choosing an image to view.

If you've followed all of the links, you should be looking at the same image that's shown in Figure 4.6.

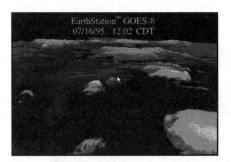

FIGURE 4.6   Cloud imagery over the Eastern United States (URL: http://www.earthwatch.com/sat2.html).

TRACING YOUR LINKS

To see where you've been, click the Back icon 3 times. On each previous page, you'll notice that the link you clicked earlier has changed color. This is how Netscape indicates home page links you've visited. By default, Netscape will maintain these link visit indicators for 30 days.

Now click the Forward icon a few times and you'll return to some of the pages you previously viewed. Did you notice that the links that took a lot longer to fully appear on your screen earlier displayed a lot more quickly this time? That's because Netscape *caches*, or stores each page you visit, during each online session, so that if you want to revisit a page, you can, in a lot less time. Unfortunately, this feature does not carry over from one session to another. Maybe in future releases it will.

Cache   A cache is a storage area. When Netscape downloads a graphic file to display, it also makes a copy of the graphic file and stores it in a directory on your hard disk. This directory is Netscape's cache. When Netscape needs to re-display the same graphic file (if you return to a previously viewed page), rather than download the graphic file again, it merely loads it from the cache directory, which allows it to display the file much faster.

In this lesson, you learned how to move through a Web page and what links are. In the next lesson, you learn how to use Netscape's History feature.

USING HISTORY TO SEE WHERE YOU'VE BEEN

In this lesson, you learn how to use Netscape's History feature.

MAKING SOME HISTORY

In Lesson 4, you learned what links are, how to find links on a Web page, and how to jump to a Web page link. What you might not have discovered yet is that Netscape keeps a trail of the Web pages you visit. This trail is called *history*.

To see how Netscape's History feature works, let's start at a Web site that has a lot of links. Let's start by visiting the Smithsonian Institution in Washington, D.C.

1. Open the File menu and choose Open Location, or click the Open button. In the Open Location dialog box, type:

   http://www.si.edu/

   This takes you to the Smithsonian home page (see Figure 5.1).

2. Click the What's New icon. Now click the link titled New and Temporary Exhibition. Scroll down to National Air and Space Museum and click this link. You should now be at the page shown in Figure 5.2.

3. Now click the link in the upper left that says National Air and Space Museum (again). When the next page appears, you will be at the National Air and Space Museum home page (see Figure 5.3).

FIGURE 5.1   Smithsonian home page.

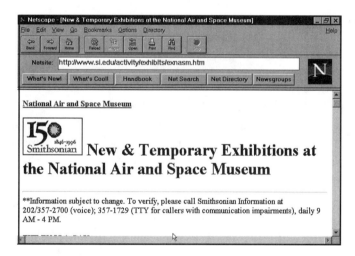

FIGURE 5.2   New and Temporary Exhibition at the National Air and Space Museum.

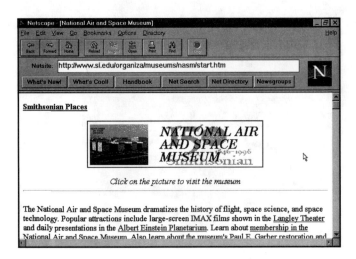

FIGURE 5.3   National Air and Space Museum home page.

4. Scroll down to the bottom of this page and click the Resources button. On the next page, scroll down to and
   click the Smithsonian Photos link.

USING THE HISTORY COMMAND

The purpose of this journey is twofold. The first is to teach you
how to use Netscape's History command. Open the Go menu and
choose View History. You should see a window similar to the one
shown in Figure 5.4.

Besides providing you with a written record of your travels on the
Net, Netscape's History feature also has a practical side. While the
History window is open, select one of the Web sites you previ-
ously visited, and click the Go to button, and then Close. Voilà!
You're back at the previous page!

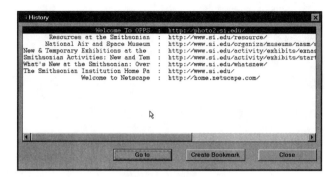

FIGURE 5.4   Netscape's History window.

If you're wondering how many history items Netscape can keep track of at one time, it depends on how much free disk space you have on your computer, and how much of that disk space you are willing to let Netscape use. Don't worry about it for now. You'll learn how Netscape makes use of your free disk space in Lesson 25, "Configuring Netscape."

The second reason for taking you on this tour of the Smithsonian is so that at the end of this lesson you can enjoy, at one of the best Web sites on the Net, some of the coolest photos of planet Earth as taken from the space shuttle.

In this lesson, you learned how to use Netscape's History feature. Unfortunately, the History feature doesn't keep a permanent record of your visits on the Net. In the next lesson, you learn how to keep a permanent record of your travels by using Netscape's Bookmark feature.

CREATING AND USING BOOKMARKS

In this lesson, you learn how to set bookmarks in Netscape and use them to return to previously visited Web sites.

UNDERSTANDING BOOKMARKS

In the last lesson, you learned that Netscape maintains a history list of Web sites you visited, and allows you to use this list to quickly jump back and forward to the sites that make up the list.

Unfortunately, this list is only temporary. It lasts only as long as your current Netscape session. All of the interesting and cool sites you visited, which were recorded in your history list, are just a distant memory when you exit Netscape.

However, Netscape does offer you a way to permanently record the URL, or location of any Web site that piqued your curiosity and held your interest. Netscape allows you to set what it calls a *bookmark.*

Bookmark A bookmark is a placeholder, whether it is something you place between the pages of a book, or something you use to track pages you have visited on the Web. In Netscape, it is a list you keep of the URLs you have visited that you would like to remember, and perhaps return to.

It is not a bookmark in the traditional sense. Netscape doesn't etch a mark in every site you visit with a cryptic note, saying something like, "Kilroy was here." Instead it records the *URL*, which is the location of the site, its name, the date you added this particular site to your bookmark list, and the last time you visited the site.

CREATING BOOKMARKS

While Netscape will automatically place Web sites in its history list, if you want Web sites placed in your bookmark list, you have to add them manually. It's a fairly simple, straightforward procedure. Let's go to three or four new sites, and place a bookmark for each:

1. Open the File menu and choose Open Location, or select the Open icon. In the Open Location dialog box, type:

    http://www.ibm.com

    This takes you to the home page of IBM (see Figure 6.1).

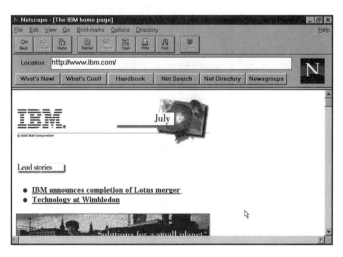

FIGURE 6.1   IBM's home page.

2. Open the Bookmarks menu and choose Add Bookmark. This places the location of the IBM home page in your bookmark list.

3. Repeat steps 1 and 2 for the following Web sites:

   • **http://networth.galt.com/dreyfus/4134/**

     This is the Dreyfus Online Information Center—a financial service firm.

   • **http://www.census.gov/**

     This is the U.S. Census Bureau.

   • **http://www.cern.ch/**

     This is CERN, The European Laboratory for Particle Physics, in Geneva, Switzerland and birthplace of the World Wide Web.

4. After you've added this list to your bookmark list, open the Bookmarks menu and choose View Bookmarks. Your list should look like the one shown in Figure 6.2.

FIGURE 6.2   Bookmark list with four Web sites added.

5. Take a look at your history list also by opening the Go menu and choosing View History; you should see the same four Web sites.

6. Exit Netscape by opening the File menu and choosing Exit.

7. Open the Start menu and choose Programs, Netscape. Then choose Netscape to restart Netscape.

8. If you open the Go menu and choose View History, you'll see that the four previously visited Web sites are not listed. But if you open the Bookmarks menu, you'll see that the four Web sites added previously are still on your list (see Figure 6.3).

FIGURE 6.3   List of bookmarks containing the previous four Web sites.

9. Choose the Census Bureau Home Page, and you'll jump back to that home page (see Figure 6.4).

FIGURE 6.4   The Census Bureau home page (URL: http://www.census.gov/).

In this lesson, you learned how to create bookmarks and use them as you surf the Net. In the next lesson, you learn how to edit and delete bookmarks.

EDITING AND DELETING BOOKMARKS

In this lesson, you learn how to edit and delete bookmarks from your list of Web pages.

EDITING BOOKMARKS

In the previous lesson, you learned how to add Web page sites to your bookmark listing as an easy means of documenting Web pages you've visited. You also saw that the advantage of including them in your bookmark list is that the bookmark list, unlike the history list, is a permanent record that remains from session to session.

The only downside to the bookmark list is that the information gathered by the bookmark function often is not very descriptive. To help remedy this deficiency, the creators of Netscape have included the capability to edit your individual bookmark listings.

Let's enter a new URL and edit its bookmark listing to illustrate this point:

1. Open the File menu and choose Open Location, or click the Open icon. The Open Location dialog box appears. Jump to the following Web page by typing:

    http://www.disney.com/

    This is the home page of Disney. As you can probably guess by looking at Figure 7.1, it is used to showcase Disney's movies.

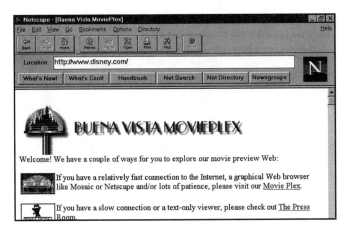

FIGURE 7.1   Buena Vista Movieplex—The Disney home page.

2. Open the Bookmarks menu and choose Add Bookmark to
    add it to your list of bookmarks.

3. Open the Bookmarks menu and choose View Bookmarks.
    This opens the Netscape Bookmarks dialog box. Select
    the bookmark Buena Vista Movieplex and choose Item,
    Properties to open the Bookmark Properties sheet (see
    Figure 7.2).

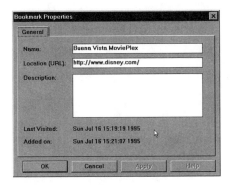

FIGURE 7.2   Bookmark Properties sheet.

4. Place the cursor in the **Name** text box. Delete Buena Vista MoviePlex and type **Disney Home Page**.

5. Place the cursor in the **Description** text box and enter a sentence or two that describes the home page. Your description can be up to 500 characters.

6. To save your changes, choose OK.

DELETING BOOKMARKS

The World Wide Web of the Internet is likely to be one of the most dynamic environments you will ever encounter. In the beginning of 1995, it was estimated that there were roughly 1 million pages on the Web. An exact count is virtually impossible since new pages are added daily, and old pages seem to change and disappear almost as fast. For this reason, and the fact that sooner or later you will probably grow tired of visiting the same group of Web pages, the creators of Netscape added a simple means of removing old Web pages from your bookmark list.

To delete the bookmark you just added:

1. Open the Bookmarks menu and choose View Bookmarks to open the Netscape Bookmarks dialog box.

2. Select the Disney Home Page bookmark.

3. Choose Edit, Delete or press the Delete key.

Reopen the bookmark list and you'll see that the listing for the Disney Home Page is gone (see Figure 7.3).

FIGURE 7.3   Disney Home Page URL removed from bookmark list.

In this lesson, you learned how to edit and delete bookmark listings. But editing and deleting alone won't make a poorly organized bookmark list easier to use, especially when you want to quickly find a particular URL in a list of several hundred. In the next lesson, you learn to organize your bookmark list.

8

ORGANIZING YOUR BOOKMARKS WITH HEADERS

In this lesson, you learn how to organize your random list of bookmarks.

UNDERSTANDING HEADERS

If you're an active Web browser, it doesn't take long before your bookmark list has a hundred or more bookmark listings. Searching through a list of a hundred or more bookmarks can be frustrating at best, or a nightmare at worst. Fortunately, there is a fairly easy and efficient method of organizing your list by creating menus.

Header In Netscape, a header is a grouping or division point of your bookmark list. The header is used to group together similar Web pages.

Here's a typical bookmark list without headers (see Figure 8.1).

As you can see, this is just a random list of bookmarks acquired from various browsing sessions. Here's the same list organized under a system of headers, which is much more structured and a lot easier to use (see Figure 8.2).

FIGURE 8.1   Bookmark list without headers.

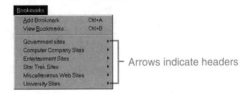

Arrows indicate headers

FIGURE 8.2   Bookmark list with headers.

CREATING HEADERS

Here's how the transformation was done in Figure 8.2. If you want to follow along using the same bookmark listings, jump to each of the Web sites listed below. At each site, choose Bookmarks, Add Bookmark and you will eventually accumulate these five sites in your Bookmarks list.

http://www.psu.edu/

http://www.cmu.edu/

http://www.pitt.edu/

http://www.purdue.edu/

http://www.ualr.edu/

1. Open the Bookmarks menu and choose View Bookmarks to open the Netscape Bookmarks dialog box.

2. Using the bookmark list shown in Figure 8.1, let's create a header called **University Sites** to group together the sites for Penn State, CMU, Pitt, Purdue, and the University of Arkansas at Little Rock. First, select the Penn State site bookmark, and choose Item, Insert Header. This opens the Bookmark Properties sheet. In the **Name** field, change **New Header** to University Sites (see Figure 8.3).

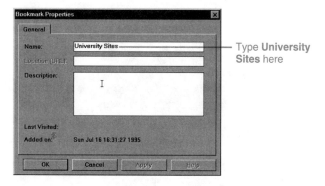

FIGURE 8.3   Creating the University Sites header.

3. Choose OK to save. In the Netscape Bookmarks dialog box, you will see that a header entitled **University Sites** has appeared under the bookmark for **Penn State** (see Figure 8.4).

4. Select the listing for Penn State by clicking and holding the left mouse button. Drag it down to the **University Sites** header, and release the mouse button. You will notice the **Penn State** listing is now indented. This indicates that it is now under and a part of the University Sites header (see Figure 8.5).

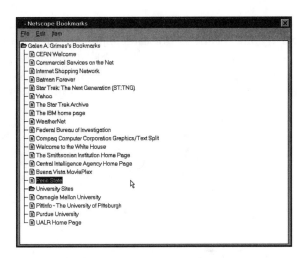

FIGURE 8.4   The University Sites menu header.

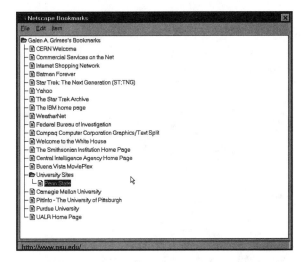

FIGURE 8.5   Penn State bookmark under University Sites header.

5. You can now drag the remaining bookmarks under the University Sites header in the same manner. You also can place them in any order you desire while dragging each bookmark to change their position. Remember, the Web sites are not grouped under the header until they are indented (see Figure 8.6).

FIGURE 8.6   All university Web sites placed under the University Sites header.

To see what the final product looks like on your Netscape menu, open the Bookmarks menu and choose University Sites. The submenu shown in Figure 8.7 pops up.

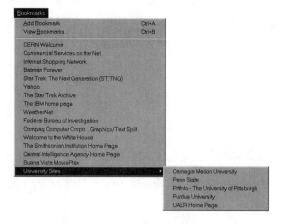

FIGURE 8.7   The University Sites submenu.

Experiment!   Experiment organizing your headers. You'll
TIP   discover that by dragging and dropping you can also
create subheaders under headers.

In this lesson, you learned how to organize your rambling list of
Web site bookmarks into a coherent, efficient listing by using
headers. In the next lesson, you learn how to find Web pages
using a keyword search.

9

SEARCHING FOR WEB SITES BY KEYWORDS

In this lesson, you learn how to search for Web sites by keywords.

WHAT IS A SEARCH ENGINE?

With more than a million Web sites in existence and new ones appearing daily, you may have begun to wonder how anyone keeps track of them, or how it's possible to locate any particular Web site or Web page. The solution to this problem is what are called *search engines*, or Web search programs. Search engines are themselves Web pages, or more precisely, they use an interactive Web page to process your search.

Search Engine   A search engine is just a fancy way of saying that it is a searchable database. The term search engine implies that besides the database, there is also a query system built-in that allows you to make your queries using common, plain English words, and not query commands.

Access to several search engines is built into Netscape. This lesson shows you how to use them. We couldn't possibly show you step-by-step how to use each one, but the instructions presented here should be sufficient to help you use the other search engines not presented in this lesson.

SEARCHING WITH LYCOS

The *Lycos* search engine, run by Carnegie Mellon University, is one of the most widely used Internet search engines. Lycos actually is two search engines: a big database search, which searches a database of more than 3.4 million Web pages; and a small database search, which searches roughly 400,000 Web pages. You decide which database to use based on how specific or obscure you think your search is. In addition to Web pages, the large Lycos database also contains information on Gopher and FTP sites (see Lessons 14 and 15 for information on using Gopher and FTP sites).

In this lesson, you will perform a search on the keywords **star trek**.

To use Lycos:

1. Click the Net Search directory button, or open the Directory menu and choose Internet Search to bring up the search engine screen (see Figure 9.1).

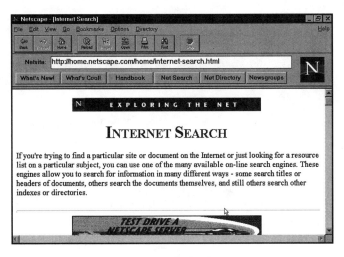

FIGURE 9.1   The Netscape search engine screen.

2. Scroll down and click the link The Lycos Home Page:
Hunting WWW Information to go to the Lycos home
page (see Figure 9.2).

FIGURE 9.2   The Lycos home page.

3. To use the big search database, which contains more than
3 million Web pages, scroll down and select the link big
Lycos catalog. To use the small database, select the link
small Lycos catalog. This takes you to the Lycos search
Web page shown in Figure 9.3.

4. In the keywords search box, type the keywords **star trek**
and press Enter. After a few seconds, the results of the
keywords search are displayed (see Figure 9.4). Keep in
mind that when you enter two or more keywords, the
database search is also done on each word individually,
which is why you see over 16,000 matches! Scroll down
through the results page to see how matches are listed.
It is up to you to ferret out the information you need.

I Got Fewer Matches!   Don't panic if the number of matches you get is greater or less than seen here. Remember, Web pages come and go all the time on the Net, so by the time you do this search, there could be more or less.

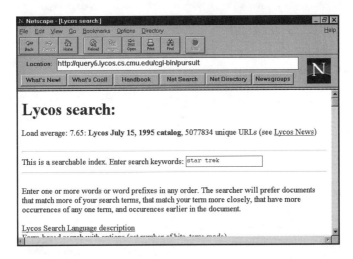

FIGURE 9.3   The Lycos search page.

As you can see, sometimes you get more information than you want, but it's a safe bet that the information you are looking for is included in this list.

Figure 9.5 helps illustrate the international aspect of the World Wide Web and the Internet. If you scroll down through this page, you will see that part of it is in Swedish. You can find this page at:

http://www.pt.hk-r.se/~pt94ero/StarTrek.html

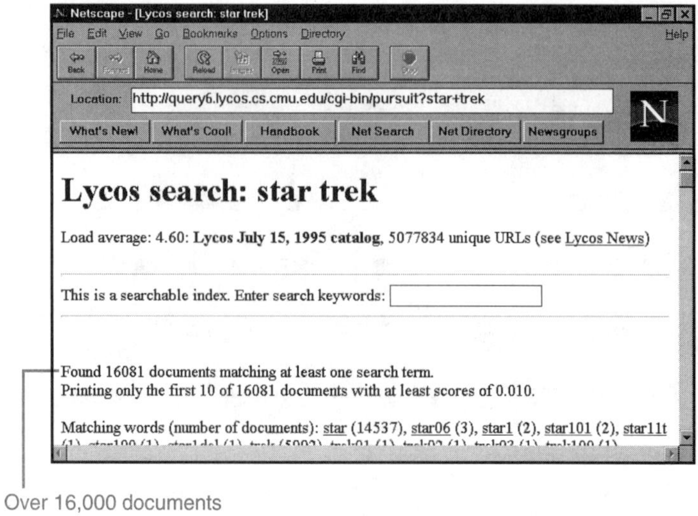

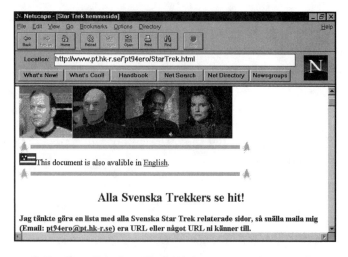

Over 16,000 documents

FIGURE 9.4   Results of the keywords search for star trek.

FIGURE 9.5   Swedish Star Trek Web page.

In this lesson, you learned how to search for Web pages by keywords. Keyword searches, however, aren't the only way to locate Web pages. In the next lesson, you learn how to search for Web pages by category.

SEARCHING FOR WEB SITES BY CATEGORY

In this lesson, you learn how to search for Web sites by category.

WHAT IS A CATEGORY?

In Lesson 9, you learned how to use some of the available Web search engines to locate Web pages based on keyword searches. But searching by keywords is not the only way to locate Web pages. A more common method is to search by category. And the most common category search tool is the Yahoo directory at Stanford University.

SEARCHING WITH YAHOO

The Yahoo directory was started by David Filo and Jerry Yang when they were graduate students at Stanford University. It now contains more than 44,000 Web page listings. Even though this is far fewer listings than Lycos, it is considered more accessible because it is organized by categories. In addition to its listing by categories, Yahoo also has a search engine that lets you search by keywords. Despite the presence of its search engine, Yahoo is covered in this lesson rather than the previous one because most of the time, Yahoo is used to ferret out Web pages by category, not by keyword. In this lesson, you learn how to use both Yahoo search methods.

SEARCH BY CATEGORY

Yahoo is primarily used for category searches. Its database is organized into the following 14 categories:

- Arts
- Business and Economy
- Computers and Internet
- Education
- Entertainment
- Government
- Health
- News
- Recreation
- Reference
- Regional
- Science
- Social Science
- Society and Culture

Obviously, if you're going to perform a search by category, you need to know which of the 14 categories your search entry falls under. To search again on **star trek**, as you did in Lesson 9 using the Lycos search engine, start under the **Entertainment** category.

Here's the search from start to finish:

1. Jump to Yahoo by clicking the Net Directory button, or by opening the Directory menu and choosing Internet Directory. This takes you to Netscape's Internet Directory page (see Figure 10.1).

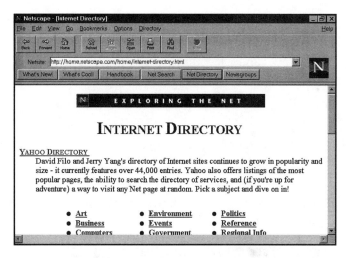

FIGURE 10.1   Netscape's Internet Directory page.

2. Click the Yahoo Directory link to jump to the Yahoo home page (see Figure 10.2).

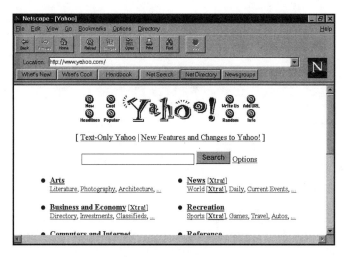

FIGURE 10.2   Yahoo home page.

3. Scroll down and select the Entertainment link to jump to the Entertainment page.

4. Scroll down and select the Television link to jump to the Entertainment:Television page.

5. Scroll down and select the Shows link to jump to the Entertainment:Television:Shows page.

6. Scroll down and select the Science Fiction link to jump to the Entertainment:Television:Shows:Science Fiction page.

7. Scroll down and select the Star Trek link to jump to the Entertainment:Television:Shows:Science Fiction:Star Trek page (see Figure 10.3).

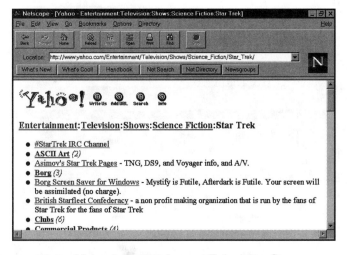

FIGURE 10.3   Yahoo's Entertainment:Television:Shows: Science Fiction:Star Trek page.

One major advantage of using Yahoo's category search database is that while you are searching for your subject, you can veer off and examine many other Web pages that fit under the search umbrella. One disadvantage, however, is that you need to have some idea of how the subject is categorized.

SEARCH BY KEYWORD

Yahoo also has a keyword search engine that you can use to search its database. It works just like the Lycos search engine described in Lesson 9. To use the Yahoo keyword search engine:

1. On the Yahoo home page, enter **star trek** in the search field.

2. Press Enter (or click the Search button) to begin the search. The results page appears (see Figure 10.4).

Click the Options Link   The **Options** link explains how to conduct more complex searches, such as using AND or OR to search on both or either keyword. This helps make your search more precise. The default search uses AND with 2 or more search keywords. In this example, that would be a search on star AND trek.

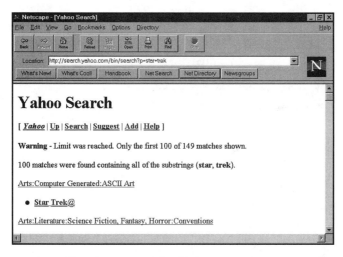

FIGURE 10.4   Results page of the Yahoo search on star trek.

In this lesson, you learned how to use one of the most popular category search tools on the World Wide Web, the Yahoo Directory. In the next lesson, you learn how to conduct geographical searches.

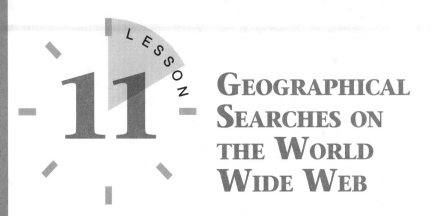

GEOGRAPHICAL SEARCHES ON THE WORLD WIDE WEB

In this lesson, you learn how to search for Web servers that are indexed under geographical databases.

WHAT ARE GEOGRAPHICAL SERVERS?

In the previous two lessons, you learned how to search for Web sites by keyword descriptions and indexed categories. Another way to locate Web servers is to search databases that are indexed by geography. These are called *geographical servers* because, as you will soon see, they are grouped by continent and country, two geographical classifications that everyone can identify with. Two such databases that are wired into Netscape are:

- World Wide Web servers at CERN

- Virtual Tourist

How Long Is It Going To Take? If you've used the other search engines available (keywords and categories), you will probably find these searches considerably slower. Part of the reason is that, in many cases, the information has a lot longer distance to travel. Many of these searches are done on other continents.

WORLD WIDE WEB SERVERS AT CERN

As stated in previous lessons, CERN, the European Laboratory for Particle Physics near Geneva, is the birthplace of the World Wide Web. It is also a repository of Web sites arranged geographically by country (and in the case of the United States, by state).

To access the CERN World Wide Web server database:

1. Click the Net Directory button, or open the Directory menu and choose Internet Directory.

2. Scroll down and select the link to the World Wide Web Servers. This takes you to the page shown in Figure 11.1.

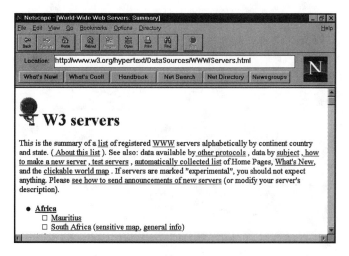

FIGURE 11.1   World Wide Web geographical server database list at CERN.

3. Scroll down the page to view the list of Web servers (links) listed by continent and country.

4. Countries listed as ***Country Name* (sensitive map, general info)** allow you to choose either a context-sensitive map, by clicking the sensitive map link (such as the one of Japan shown in Figure 11.2), or a text listing of

the available Web servers in that country (as shown in Figure 11.3), which you get by selecting the general info
link. If all you see is the name of the country, only a
text listing of that country's Web servers is available.
Figure 11.4 shows the general info listing of the Web
servers in Hong Kong posted on a server at the Chinese
University of Hong Kong.

Context-Sensitive Map A context-sensitive map is
merely a map that will give you different results depending on where you click it. You may have to experiment to
get a "feel" for where you need to click each map.

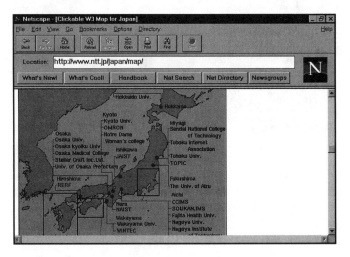

FIGURE 11.2 Context-sensitive Web server map of Japan.

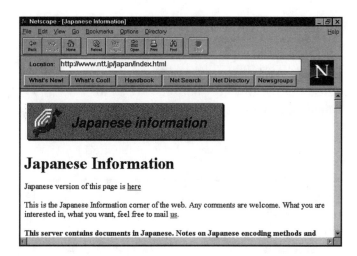

FIGURE 11.3   Japanese Web server.

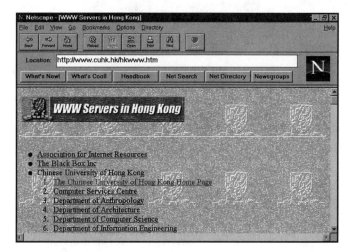

FIGURE 11.4   Listing of Web servers in Hong Kong.

VIRTUAL TOURIST

The Virtual Tourist is the other popular geographical Web server database. To access the Virtual Tourist:

1. Click the Net Directory button, or open the Directory menu and choose Internet Directory.

2. Scroll down and select the link marked Virtual Tourist. This takes you to the page shown in Figure 11.5.

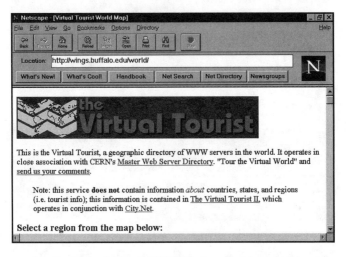

FIGURE 11.5   Virtual Tourist WWW geographical database.

The Virtual Tourist is similar in operation to the database at CERN, except that you start out with a map of the world.

3. Scroll down the current page to access the map shown in Figure 11.6.

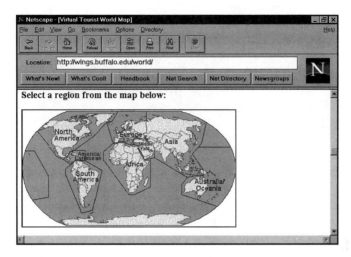

FIGURE 11.6   Virtual Tourist context-sensitve map.

4. Clicking a continent will cause you to jump to a continent map. Clicking a country will cause you to jump to a country map (or text listing, if a map is not available). Depending on the country and concentration of Web servers in that country, your next jump will either be to a region (or state) in that country or to a Web server in that country.

Because both databases are, in essence, listings of the same Web servers, eventually you will jump to the same servers as you did in the CERN database.

In this lesson, you learned how to use two popular databases to find servers located in geographical areas of the world. In the next lesson, you learn how to search for users and their e-mail addresses on the Internet.

SEARCHING FOR PEOPLE ON THE INTERNET

In this lesson, you learn how to search for people on the Internet.

LOCATING PEOPLE ON THE INTERNET

Even though Netscape is plugged in to several user search engines, currently, searching for people on the Internet is more of a promise than a reality. This is partly because there is no central registration repository of usernames and e-mail addresses.

FOUR11 DIRECTORY SERVICE

Possibly the best method for searching for other users on the Internet is the Four11 Directory Service search engine. Its major drawback is that before you can use it to find someone, you need to register yourself with Four11 to gain access to its search database. Also, the person you are looking for has to register with Four11 to be included in its database search. The basic Four11 service is free, but Four11 also has a paid service, which gives you a few more search parameters. This lesson only examines the free Four11 service.

 Security Alert   When registering and searching using Four11, be aware that you are passing information over the Internet in an insecure method, meaning that it can be intercepted and read. Don't pass confidential information, such as credit card information, passwords, and so on. By default, Netscape warns you in advance that you are passing insecure information.

Here's how Four11 works:

1. Open the Directory menu and choose Internet White Pages to go to the People and Places page.

2. Scroll down the page to the Four11 Directory Service link and select it. This takes you to the Four11 home page (see Figure 12.1).

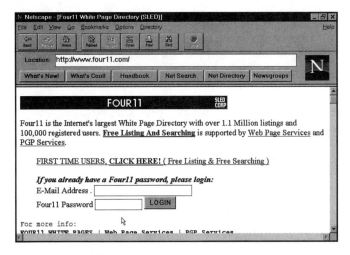

FIGURE 12.1   The Four11 Directory Service.

3. If you are not registered with Four11, you are encouraged to do so by selecting the FIRST TIME USERS CLICK HERE! link. Select this link and jump to the Four11 registration page.

4. Scroll down the page and fill in the boxes for:

   • First & Middle Names

   • Last Name

   • Optional Prefix/Suffix (such as Dr., Sir., Jr., Sr., and so on)

   • Location: City, State/Province, Country

- Internet Address

- Two additional e-mail addresses

- An old e-mail address

- The URL of your Web page, if you have one

- Three optional Group Organizations

5. When you have completed the form, select the Submit Form button to submit your registration form to Four11. Within a day, Four11 will respond back to you via e-mail indicating that you are registered, and issue you a password for its service.

After you have registered with Four11, here's how to search for someone (who, hopefully, is also registered):

 Free Search!   Four11 will take a day (at least) to send you your password. However, if you don't feel like waiting, after you register, you can click the Click HERE to search the directory link to begin searching for other Internet users.

1. Open the Directory menu and choose Internet White Pages to go to the People and Places page.

2. Scroll down the page to the Four11 Directory Service link and select it. This takes you to the Four11 home page.

3. Enter your e-mail address and the password Four11 issued you. Select the LOGIN button. This takes you to the Four11 search page (see Figure 12.2).

4. Click the SEARCH Directory link. This takes you to the Four11 search input page (see Figure 12.3).

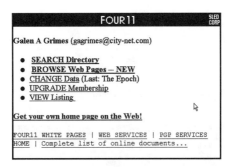

FIGURE 12.2   The Four11 search page.

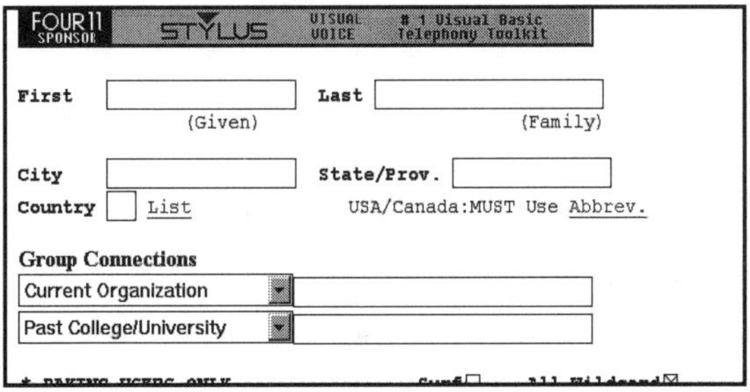

FIGURE 12.3   The Four11 search input page.

5. Enter as much information as you can about the person you are searching for (name, city, state, country, and so on) and select Search.

   For this example, search for the author by entering **Galen** in the **First** field, **Grimes** in the **Last** field, **Pittsburgh** in the **City** field, **PA** in the **State/Prov.** field, and **US** in the **Country** field.

6. Within a few seconds, Figure 12.4 appears displaying the listing on Four11.

7. The listing appears as a link. When you click it, the full listing appears (see Figure 12.5).

```
SUCCESSFUL SEARCH, MATCHES: 1 (click on listings for additional details)

GIVEN NAMES      FAMILY NAME      E-MAIL ADDRESS
--------------   ----------------  --------------------
Galen A          Grimes            gagrimes@city-net.com
```

FIGURE 12.4   Four11 listing for author.

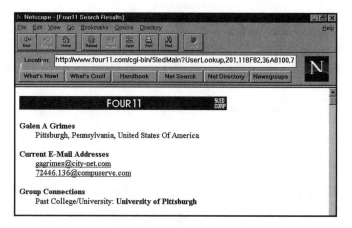

FIGURE 12.5   Full Four11 listing for author.

When I tried using Four11 to search for several of the editors at Macmillan Computer Publishing, some were found and some weren't, which confirms my earlier fault with this system; you have to register with it.

In this lesson, you learned how to use what's currently considered the best method of obtaining someone's e-mail address, short of asking him for it. In the next lesson, you learn how to find new and cool sites on the World Wide Web.

SEARCHING FOR NEW & COOL WEB SITES

In this lesson, you learn how to locate many new and cool Web sites on the World Wide Web.

USING WHAT'S NEW!

By some estimates, the World Wide Web gets several hundred new Web pages each week. Trying to locate and examine each one could easily be a full-time job. But, fortunately, there are ways to get information about new pages. There are organizations that screen new pages and keep lists of which ones the majority of Web browsers might find interesting.

In Netscape, one of its six directory buttons is configured to help you locate new Web pages. Netscape developers post and update the Netscape What's New? Web page. To find out what's new:

1. Click the What's New! directory button, or open the Directory menu and choose What's New to access Netscape's What's New? Web page.

2. Scroll down the page to view the new Web page links (see Figure 13.1).

The Yahoo Web site (covered in Lesson 10, "Searching for Web Sites by Category") also keeps a What's New on Yahoo page that has a link on the Netscape What's New? page.

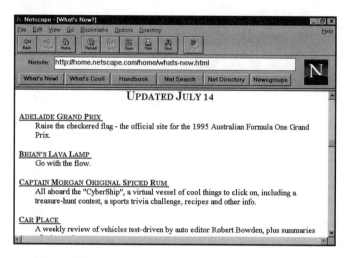

FIGURE 13.1 What's New? Web page links—subject to change, frequently.

1. Scroll down to and click the What's New on Yahoo link on Netscape's What's New? page (see Figure 13.2). This takes you to the What's New Yahoo page.

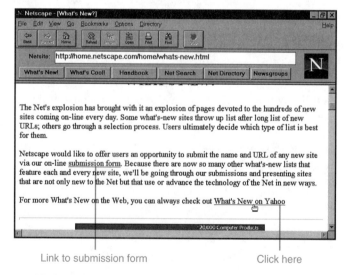

Link to submission form   Click here

FIGURE 13.2 What's New on Yahoo link.

2. The Yahoo What's New page keeps a listing of new Web pages listed in its database during the previous week, arranged by day. Select any or all of the links to take a look at some of the new pages recently posted on the Yahoo database.

Netscape's developers are always looking for new Web pages; they even provide a submission form in case you find one or two they miss.

1. Scroll down Netscape's What's New? page until you see Netscape's submission form link (see Figure 13.2). Click this link to go to Netscape's Tell Us What's New form (see Figure 13.3).

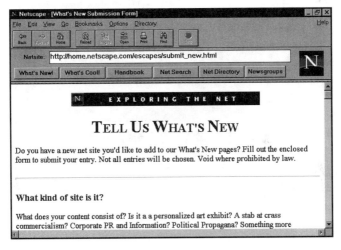

FIGURE 13.3   Netscape's new Web site submission form.

2. Scroll down the page and fill in the blanks to supply information such as what type of Web site it is, its URL and title, and someone to contact if any additional information is needed.

USING WHAT'S COOL!

If you spent any time looking at many of the Web pages under the various What's New listings, you probably yawned a lot. Many are interesting and some contain a lot of useful information, but let's face it, some are quite boring as well.

Despite the fact that the Internet was originally created for government and academia, not all of the information you'll run across is rocket science, economic briefings, or quantum physics. There are a lot of really cool Web pages out there. Once again, the developers of Netscape have taken the initiative in helping you find them by providing a **What's Cool!** directory button.

1. Click the What's Cool! button, or open the Directory menu and choose What's Cool!. This takes you to Netscape's What's Cool? page (see Figure 13.4).

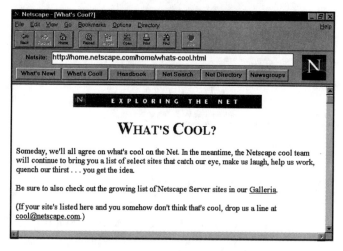

FIGURE 13.4   Netscape's What's Cool? page.

2. Scroll down the page and select the links that interest you. Some cool sites we recommend include:

- The 48th Cannes International Film Festival

  http://www.interactive8.com:80/cannes/ welcome/welcome.html

- Kodak (they have breath-taking pictures)

  http://www.kodak.com/

- MTV, Music Television

  http://www.mtv.com/

- Virtual Hawaii (if you can't vacation there, stop by this Web site)

  http://www.satlab.hawaii.edu/space/hawaii

- Tahiti

  http://www.inch.com/~stuartb/tahiti.htm

- The Trivia Page

  http://www.primate.wisc.edu/homepage/ d.hamel/trivia.html

Obviously, any listing claiming to show what's cool is going to be highly subjective, even a listing generated by Netscape's own team. Netscape has set up a feedback system. If you disagree with its definition of what's cool, you can send them comments via e-mail to **cool@netscape.com**.

In this lesson, you learned how to use Netscape's What's New! and What's Cool! directory buttons to locate new and cool Web sites. In the next lesson, you learn how to access Gopher servers on the Internet.

14

ACCESSING GOPHER SERVERS AND USING VERONICA

In this lesson, you learn how to access Gopher servers using Netscape.

WHAT IS A GOPHER SERVER?

So far, everything you've seen and every place you've been on the Internet has been in a graphical context. But as you'll soon see, there's a large part of the Internet that has no pictures, no icons, no colors, and no sounds. It's the part of the Internet that was around before the World Wide Web was created. It's the part that is made up of text-based menus and text-only files. And the first part of it you'll explore using Netscape is the world of *gopherspace*.

Gopherspace Gopherspace is the collective term used to describe the interconnection of Gopher servers. As you will soon see, Gopher servers often have interconnecting links in their menus, much the same way Web pages have links to other Web pages.

A *Gopher server* is a system made up of hierarchical text-based menus arranged by subject. As you dig deeper through Gopher menus, you will eventually find text screens or text files. Gophers tend to be good places to locate a lot of information by subject, such as government statistics, catalogues, and general information on a variety of subjects. Some Gophers contain information that has not been touched in 10 years or more, such as university research projects or experiments.

USING NETSCAPE TO BROWSE GOPHERS

When you use Netscape to browse text-based Gopher systems, you'll notice that it can't seem to break away from its graphical nature. Netscape places an icon in front of each item in a Gopher menu to explain what you will encounter if you choose that selection. Here is a brief explanation of what each icon represents:

ICON	DESCRIPTION
Menu	Represents another menu you can jump to. This menu can be on the same Gopher server, or it can be a link to another Gopher server.
Text document	Eventually, all Gopher menus lead to text files.
Binary file	This is a binary (non-text) file that is usually accessed via FTP (FTP servers are explained in Lesson 15). These are often very large text files that have been compressed so as to take up less space on a server and, therefore, download quicker.
Telnet session	Telnet sessions are text-based sessions run on remote mainframe computers that operate text-based programs.
Gopher search	Used to initiate a Gopher search. Type the subject you want to search on. Based on the search criteria, you are usually taken to a new Gopher menu.

Now that you know what to expect to find on a Gopher server, let's see how it works:

1. Open the File menu and choose Open Location, or click the Open button on the toolbar. In the Open Location dialog box, enter:

   gopher://gopher.micro.umn.edu

   You should be at the Gopher server shown in Figure 14.1.

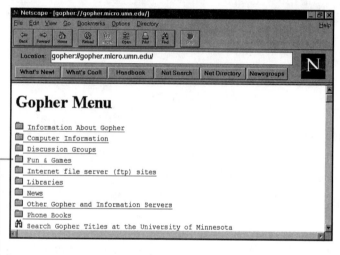

Click here

FIGURE 14.1   Gopher server of the University of Minnesota.

2. Click the menu icon next to the **Fun & Games** link.

3. Click the menu icon next to the **Movies** link to go to the movie review menu (see Figure 14.2).

4. Click the Gopher search icon next to the **Search Movie Archives** link. The Gopher Search screen appears. In the keywords field, enter **james bond** (see Figure 14.3).

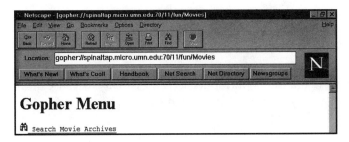

FIGURE 14.2   Movie review Gopher site.

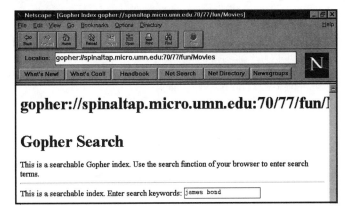

FIGURE 14.3   Gopher Search screen.

The results of the Gopher search on the keywords **james bond** appear.

If you want to find out why so many movies appear on this list that are apparently not part of the James Bond series, click one of the documents. Then, open the Edit menu and choose Find. In the Find dialog box, enter **james bond** to do a search on these words. You'll find that these two words appear somewhere in the text.

5. Click the document fun/Movies/1987/Aug/ THE LIVING DAYLIGHTS to see the review of the James Bond film, *The Living Daylights*.

ACCESSING AND SEARCHING WITH VERONICA

Veronica, a program that indexes Gopher menus, is a search engine operating on a Gopher server. (Actually, because of the popularity of Veronica, there are numerous Veronica Gopher servers you can use.)

 Veronica   The name Veronica is an acronym for Very Easy Rodent Oriented Net-wide Index of Computerized Archives. However, this is just one explanation. The other, more popular explanation is that Veronica is named after one of the girlfriends of the comic strip character Archie (Archie is the name of another archive searching program used for searching FTP sites).

To access Veronica:

1. Open the File menu and choose Open Location, or click the Open button on the toolbar. In the Open Location dialog box, enter:

    gopher://veronica.scs.unr.edu/11/veronica

    This takes you to the Gopher server shown in Figure 14.4.

 Nothing Happens!   Don't panic if you attempt to jump to this Gopher server and nothing happens. This is a very popular and very busy Gopher server, so you may not always connect. If this happens, either wait a few minutes and try again, or try using one of the alternative Veronica Gopher servers listed at the end of this lesson.

2. Select the search icon next to the **Simplified veronica: Find gopher MENUS only** link. This takes you to the query page shown in Figure 14.5.

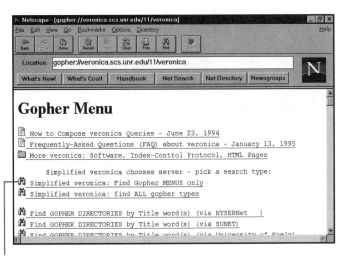

Click here

FIGURE 14.4   Veronica Gopher server.

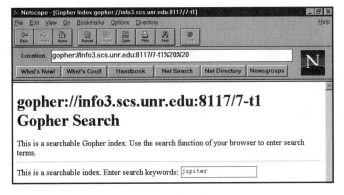

FIGURE 14.5   Veronica query page.

3. Type your query keyword and press Enter. For this example, use the keyword **jupiter.** Within a minute, the
   results of your query appear on-screen (see Figure 14.6).

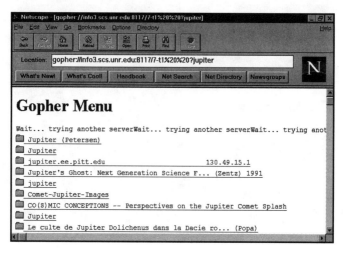

FIGURE 14.6   Query results.

This is a basic Veronica search. As you become more comfortable
using Gopher, read the files posted on how to conduct Veronica
queries, and the Frequently Asked Questions (FAQ) to learn how
to expand your Gopher searches and use more complicated keyword queries. Below are some interesting Veronica Gophers to
jump to:

- gopher://liberty.uc.wlu.edu/11/gophers/
  veronica

- gopher://info.psi.net:2347/7

- gopher://pulsar.tach.net:2347/7

- gopher://veronica.unipi.it:2347/7

In this lesson, you learned how to use Netscape to "go-fer" information in a Gopher server and how to use Veronica to search for
Gopher servers. In the next lesson, you learn how to use Netscape
to access FTP servers.

ACCESSING FTP SERVERS

15

In this lesson, you learn how to use Netscape to access FTP servers on the Internet.

WHAT IS AN FTP SERVER?

In the last lesson, you learned that not all sites on the Internet are graphical Web servers; you learned about text-based Gopher servers, which are repositories of text files that store factual information. These text files are often arranged under hierarchical menu systems that help categorize the information for which you are looking.

Like Gopher servers, FTP servers are text-based and contain files for your use. But unlike Gopher servers, FTP servers don't come equipped with well-organized menus, and the files found on them are mostly program files, not text files.

FTP FTP stands for *File Transfer Protocol*. It is a means by which Internet computers communicate with each other, exchange files, and pass updated lists. For the purposes of this lesson, it is the program and the means used to exchange files with an Internet computer.

FTP servers are often used by computer hardware and software vendors to distribute software and updates to their customers. In fact, you probably got the copy of Netscape you are running now off the Netscape FTP server. You might also hear the term *anonymous FTP* used to describe FTP servers. FTP servers originally were used to transfer files from one user to another, which required a login ID and password. When FTP servers were "opened" to the public, it was decided that everyone's ID would be *anonymous*, and the user's password would be his e-mail address. Netscape enters these for you when you use it to access an FTP server.

How To Access an FTP Server

To jump to an FTP server, enter its URL the same as you would for a Web server or a Gopher server. Web servers all begin with **http://**, Gopher servers all begin with **gopher://**, and FTP servers all begin with **ftp://**. Let's take a look at Netscape's FTP server:

1. Open the File menu and choose Open Location, or click the Open button on the toolbar. In the Open Location dialog box, enter:

   ftp://ftp.netscape.com

   This takes you to the Netscape FTP server (see Figure 15.1). (If the Netscape FTP server looks somewhat different, don't be alarmed. Directories are sometimes added and/or deleted.)

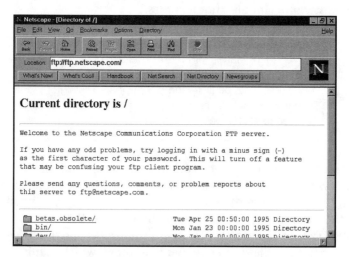

Figure 15.1   Netscape's FTP server.

2. Scroll down the page until you see the complete directory
   listing (folder icons).

Just as you encountered a series of icons on Gopher servers, you
will likewise see icons that represent different items on an FTP
server.

ICON		DESCRIPTION
	subdirectory	A directory dependent to the one you're currently in. A subdirectory can contain files or more subdirectories.
	document	A file containing an HTML or PostScript file that you can transfer to your computer.
	generic file	A file of some unspecified type.
	program file	A program file or a compressed archive file containing executable program files, such as Netscape for Windows, which is listed as **n16e11n.exe**.

NAVIGATING THROUGH AN FTP SERVER

Because FTP servers are made up of directories and subdirectories
similar to the folders and subfolders on your PC, you will need to
know how to navigate through them using Netscape. Clicking an
FTP subdirectory icon takes you to a hierarchical storage level
below the one you are currently at. This is the same as using the
Windows 95 Explorer to traverse several layers of folders on
your computer's hard disk.

To go back up to the next higher level, you need to scroll up until you see a link that says:

Up to higher level directory

Clicking this link takes you up a directory level. When you can no longer find this link, it means you are at the highest level you are permitted to access.

TRANSFERRING A FILE FROM AN FTP SERVER

Accessing an FTP server is merely the first part of the puzzle. To make use of an FTP server, you need to transfer, or download, a file to your computer. With Netscape, this is as easy as pointing and clicking.

 Virus Alert!   Be aware that when you access an FTP server, you are potentially exposing your computer to computer viruses. Most server administrators scan all files that come into their servers, but occasionally some infected files do get in. Always make sure you are running an up-to-date anti-virus program before you download files.

1. Open the File menu and choose Open Location, or click the Open button on the toolbar. In the Open Location dialog box, enter the following FTP site:

    ftp://ftp.wustl.edu

    This is the FTP server operated by Washington University in St. Louis.

Could Not Log In to FTP Server! FTP servers often have limits as to the number of users who can log in at one time. When that limit is reached, as will often happen on very popular servers, it will not permit any additional logins. If you get an error message similar to this, don't panic. Just try again later.

2. At the Washington University FTP site (see Figure 15.2), scroll down to and click the directory icon pub/.

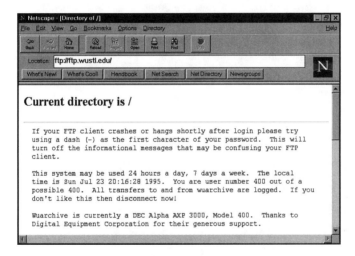

FIGURE 15.2   The Washington University FTP server.

3. Scroll down to the WINDOWS_UPLOADS/ icon. Click this icon to descend into this subdirectory.

4. Scroll down until you see the file fbclck46.zip. Click this file to download it to your computer.

File Not Found!   FTP servers and their contents do occasionally change; it's possible that after storing a file for a certain period of time, the administrator has removed it.

 Eliminate Steps   To save some time downloading the file, if you already know the file's name and location, include it in the URL you enter in the Open Location dialog box. For example, had you entered:

ftp://ftp.wustl.edu/pub/WINDOWS_UPLOADS/ fbclck46.zip

you would have eliminated several of the steps listed here.

5. Netscape should then present a warning dialog box indicating that this is an unknown file type, and asking you how you wish to proceed (see Figure 15.3). Click Save to Disk to begin the download.

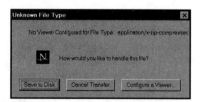

Figure 15.3   Netscape's Unknown File Type dialog box.

The file you just downloaded is a Windows clock that you can configure with the face of your favorite football team. If you want to see what this program looks like and how it works, download and install it.

Got a Copy of PKUNZIP?   Many files you find on FTP servers will have the file extension ZIP. This means that it is a compressed file archive. To decompress files of this type, you need a program called PKUNZIP. If you don't have a copy of PKUNZIP, you can get a copy at **ftp:// oak.oakland.edu in pub/pc-blue/util**.

In this lesson, you learned how to transfer files to your computer from FTP servers. In the next lesson, you learn how to locate files and FTP servers using Archie.

16

LESSON

LOCATING FILES AND FTP SERVERS USING ARCHIE

In this lesson, you learn how to locate files on FTP servers using Archie.

WHAT IS ARCHIE?

The *Archie system* is an archival retrieval system designed to continually maintain its database of files stored in FTP servers. There are some who even believe that the name Archie is a derivative of "archive," even though there is no proof to substantiate this claim. The Archie system of databases is the direct result of the early planning—similar to the planning that went into the searches done on Gopher servers (see Lesson 14)—that went into indexing FTP servers and maintaining databases of the files they contain. As a result, the files could be quickly located. The problem with indexing FTP servers is more acute, however, because there are probably 20 times more files on FTP servers than there are menus on Gopher servers.

Worldwide, there are a series of Archie servers that do nothing but constantly search FTP sites in their geographical region to keep their databases up-to-date. They, in turn, exchange the results of their database searches with other Archie servers. The bottom line is that, approximately every 20 days, each Archie server should be updated on the contents of other Archie servers.

LOCATING FTP SERVERS AND FILES

To begin your FTP search, you need to jump to a Web page that has links to Archie sites worldwide.

1. Open the File menu and choose Open Location, or click the Open button on the toolbar. In the Open Location dialog box, enter:

    http://web.nexor.co.uk/archie.html

    This takes you to the Web page shown in Figure 16.1. (To find out more about Archie servers and how they work, be sure to check out the **Public Service**, **NEXOR**, and **Archie** links.)

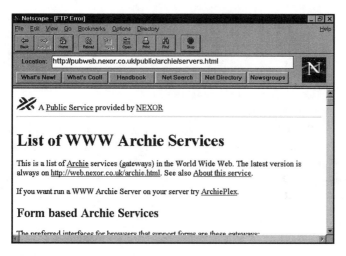

FIGURE 16.1   List of WWW Archie Services.

2. Scroll down and select an Archie server. Selecting one on your same continent generally results in a faster search. For this example, choose the Archie server AA at NCSA in the United States.

3. In the Archie Request Form, enter the name of the file you wish to find. If you're not sure of the name, you can enter just the first few letters of the file name. For this

example, search for **pk204g.exe** (see Figure 16.2). This
is the archived version of PKZIP, a fairly common file
compression program.

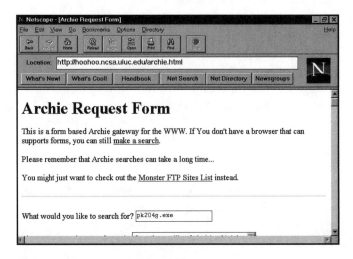

FIGURE **16.2** Archie Request Form.

4. Scroll down to the **There are several types of search**
   field. Select Case Insensitive Substring Match, if it is not
   already selected. This search type broadens your search
   parameters.

5. In the **The results can be sorted by** field, decide how
   you want the search results (files located) sorted by selecting the By Host or By Date radio button. **By Host** sorts
   the files according to the names of the FTP servers where
   they are found. This can often provide you with a list of
   servers closer to you, which will download faster. **By
   Date** sorts the results by file date (which is usually the
   date it was placed on the FTP server, but which also can
   indicate how old the file is).

6. In the **The impact on other users can be** field, decide how much impact you want to place on other users. This means you can choose whether to fairly share the Archie server's system resources with other users who are conducting searches, or hog the resources so that the Archie server applies more of its resources to conducting your search. You decide how nice you want to be.

7. If you decide to use other Archie servers, you may have to experiment with the settings in the **Several Archie Servers can be used** field to determine which selection produces the best search results.

8. In the **You can restrict the number of results returned** field, the default number of file locations returned is **10**. Leave this number as is, until you have more experience with Archie searches.

9. Select the Submit button to begin your search. In a few moments, the results of your search will be displayed (see Figure 16.3).

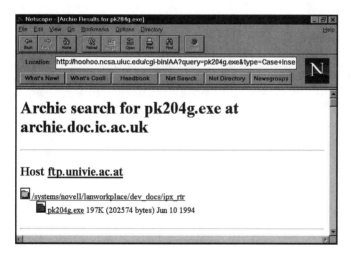

FIGURE 16.3   Results of Archie search.

10. Scroll down the results page. You'll find that even though your substring search produced a lot of "misses" (not found, or found incorrect file), you also got a few "hits" (found correct file).

In this lesson, you learned the basics of searching FTP sites using Archie. As with most of the other search engines, to get the best results for your needs, you will have to experiment with the various parameters. In the next lesson, you learn how to use Netscape to access Internet newsgroups.

CONFIGURING AND ACCESSING USENET NEWSGROUPS

In this lesson, you learn how to use Netscape to access UseNet newsgroups.

WHAT ARE USENET NEWSGROUPS?

Newsgroups are, in effect, electronic discussion groups. In these groups, users discuss various topics ranging from aviation and alien visitors to Zen and zoology. Each of the 10,000 or more newsgroups usually limits discussion to just one topic.

Even though they are single-topic by definition, as you browse through a few newsgroups, you'll see that a topic can have many sides, or *threads*. Threads are discussed more in the next lesson.

UseNet The term UseNet predates the Internet. It refers to an early system of connecting mainframe computers using standard telephone lines and crude versions of desktop modems to transfer discussion articles.

CONFIGURING NETSCAPE FOR NEWSGROUPS

Before you can access any of the Internet newsgroups, you need to make some configurations in Netscape.

1. Open the Options menu and choose Preferences. The
   Preferences dialog box appears. Select the Mail and News
   tab and you will see the screen displayed in Figure 17.1.

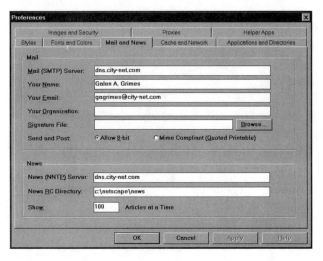

FIGURE 17.1   Preferences dialog box.

2. In the **News (NNTP) Server** field, enter the name of
   your news server. If you are not sure, contact your system
   administrator or Internet Service Provider (ISP).

3. In the **News RC Directory** field, enter a folder
   (directory) on your computer in which you can store
   newsgroup and subscription files produced while you are
   accessing your server's newsgroups.

4. Choose OK to save your changes.

ACCESSING NEWSGROUPS

Now that you've configured Netscape, to access newsgroups:

1. Click the Newsgroups directory button. You'll jump to
   a page that shows you which newsgroups you have
   subscribed to (see Figure 17.2).

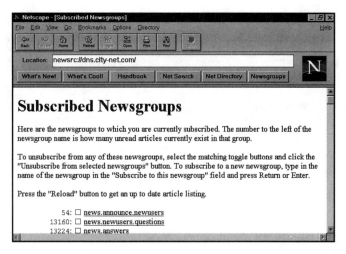

FIGURE 17.2   News server list.

2. The first time you access newsgroups, you are automatically subscribed to three newsgroups:

   • **news.announce.newusers**

   • **news.newusers.questions**

   • **news.answers**

3. To see the other newsgroups available, scroll down to and click the View all newsgroups button. The Newsgroups list appears (see Figure 17.3).

Your Newsgroups List Looks Different?   There are no standards for which newsgroups have to be kept on every news server. Your administrator may not keep newsgroup lists as long as some others.

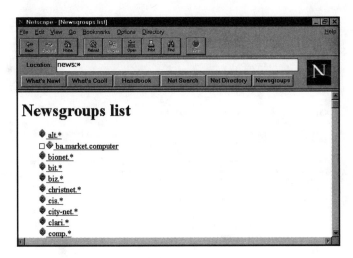

FIGURE 17.3   Newsgroups list.

In this lesson, you learned how to configure Netscape for
newsgroups and how to access newsgroups on your news server.
In the next lesson, you learn how to read and respond to news
items and how to subscribe to newsgroups.

READING AND SUBSCRIBING TO NEWSGROUPS

In this lesson, you learn about using newsgroups—how to read news items and how to subscribe to newsgroups.

HOW NEWSGROUPS ARE ORGANIZED

Newsgroups are divided into seven major categories:

- **alt** (alternative) Topics fall outside of the mainstream; some are very controversial.

- **comp.** (computers) These topics are concerned with computers and computer science.

- **news** (newsgroups) News about newsgroups and their operations.

- **rec.** (recreational) Topics deal with recreational interests.

- **sci.** (science) Focuses on scientific issues.

- **soc.** (social) This group encompasses social issues.

- **talk** Focuses on the aspects of a public debating forum.

Besides these seven major groupings, many news servers also maintain a number of minor groups, such as biz (business), bionet (biology), courts, general, misc. (miscellaneous), and humor. There are countless others you can encounter too, so you should be able to find a topic that's of interest to you.

Oh My Gosh, Everyone's an Expert, Except Me!
Nothing could be further from the truth. One important thing to keep in mind is that you will often encounter users who try to pass themselves off as experts on a given topic. They will toss out (supposed) facts and unbelievable statistics to bolster their arguments. Don't take all of it at face value.

READING NEWS ITEMS

Here's where the fun starts. Scroll down through your list of newsgroups until you find one that interests you. In this example, you're going to select a newsgroup and find an article to read.

1. Click the alt. link to reveal the subgroups under the alternative category (see Figure 18.1).

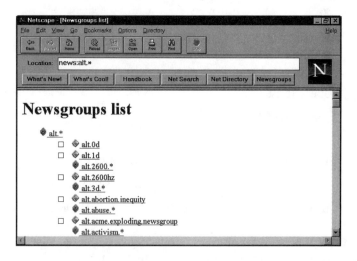

FIGURE 18.1   alt. subgroups.

2. Scroll down through the list of alt. subgroups to alt.comedy and click this group.

3. Click alt.comedy.standup to reveal the list of articles (see Figure 18.2).

Response appears indented under bulleted link

FIGURE 18.2   alt.comedy.standup articles.

4. To read an article, click a bulleted link and the article appears (see Figure 18.3).

FIGURE 18.3   Article on stand-up comedians.

Responses to articles appear under the bulleted link (refer to Figure 18.2). Responses are indented to indicate their dependence on the primary article.

SUBSCRIBING TO NEWSGROUPS

Subscribing to newsgroups ensures that Netscape will help keep track of all incoming and read articles. It does not post your name on a mailing list for junk mail, make you a member of any group, or obligate you to purchase anything. It is just a way of helping you keep track of the discussions occurring in the group or groups you designate.

To subscribe to a newsgroup:

1. Go back to the newsgroup you want to subscribe to. In the previous example, it would be **alt.comedy.standup**.

2. Place an **X** in the box to the left of the newsgroup (see Figure 18.4) by clicking in the box.

FIGURE 18.4   Subscribing to alt.comedy.standup.

3. Click the Subscribe to selected newsgroups button. The newsgroup you subscribed to now appears on the list

with the three you subscribed to by default (see Figure 18.5).

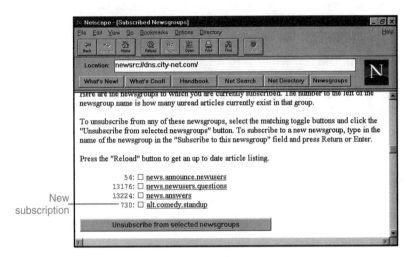

New subscription

FIGURE 18.5   List of subscribed newsgroups.

4. If (or when) you want to unsubscribe to a newsgroup, just select the newsgroup from the list of subscribed newsgroups shown in Figure 18.5. Click in the box to place an **X** next to the newsgroup you want to unsubscribe. Then click the Unsubscribe from selected newsgroups button.

If you have a strong interest in newsgroups, perhaps you should look into acquiring a better newsgroup reader.

Use a Better Newsreader   Netscape is okay for occasional browsing, but WinVN, a shareware program that can be found on numerous FTP sites under the file name **winvn.zip**, is a much better tool for the serious newsgroup junkie.

You might also consider investigating newsgroups and their operation beyond the cursory overview presented here. There are numerous books written on the single topic of newsgroups, such as Que's *Using UseNet Newsgroups*, that explain in greater detail how to use every facet of this Internet resource.

In this lesson, you learned how to read newsgroup articles and how to subscribe to newsgroups. In the next lesson, you learn how to use Netscape to send e-mail to other Internet users.

SENDING E-MAIL USING NETSCAPE

LESSON 19

In this lesson, you learn how to use Netscape to send e-mail to other Internet users.

WHAT IS E-MAIL?

E-mail, short for electronic mail, is one of the oldest uses of the Internet. It still remains one of the major reasons why people go online.

E-mail is fast. It usually arrives in less than a day, depending on the distance it must travel and whether it encounters any delays because of network trouble spots. In many cases, e-mail originating and being delivered in the U.S. will arrive in several minutes. And depending on your Internet service provider, it usually costs nothing beyond your normal monthly service fee.

CONFIGURING NETSCAPE TO SEND E-MAIL

Before you can use Netscape to send e-mail, you must tell Netscape a little bit about yourself and configure the program to work with your local mail server.

To configure Netscape:

1. Open the Options menu and choose Preferences. In the Preferences dialog box, click the Mail and News tab. Your screen should look like the one in Figure 19.1.

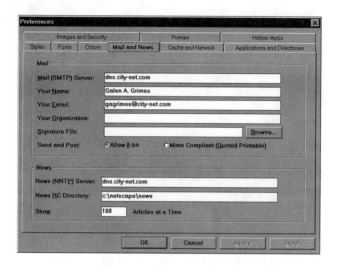

FIGURE 19.1   Mail and News Preferences dialog box.

2. In the **Mail (SMTP) Server** field, enter the name of your local mail server. If you're not sure, contact your system administrator or Internet Service Provider (ISP).

3. In the **Your Name** field, enter your name as you want it to appear on e-mail messages (Galen A. Grimes, Gen. Colin Powell, Amb. Sarek, and so on).

4. In the **Your Email** field, enter your e-mail address. It should be in the form *userid@mail.server*, where userid is the login ID assigned to you by your system administrator or ISP, and *mail.server* is the name of your local mail server. Again, if you're not sure, contact your system administrator or ISP.

5. In the **Your Organization** field, enter an organization name. (This is optional.)

6. In the **Signature File** field, enter the drive, path, and file name of the text file that contains your e-mail signature. (This is optional.)

    The **Browse** button next to the **Signature File** field allows you to browse through the directories on your hard disk if you are not exactly sure where your signature file is located.

E-Mail Signature An e-mail signature is a short saying, phrase, or thought you wish to convey. It is usually one line in length, and might say something like:

"Live long and prosper."

"Elvis lives!"

"Don't get mad, get even."

"Save the rain forests."

The only firm rule for using a signature is to keep it short.

7. At the final configuration choice, **Send and Post**, select the Allow 8-bit radio button (the default).

If you are going to be sending messages with a variety of binary file attachments (such as audio files, encapsulated messages, video files, or graphic images) and you are certain that the recipient is using an e-mail program that is MIME-compliant, select the **Mime Compliant** (Multipurpose Internet Mail Extension) radio button instead.

8. Choose OK to close the Preferences dialog box. Then open the Options menu and choose Save Options to save the information you just entered.

Sending E-Mail

Once you get Netscape configured, you can send your first e-mail message. To send a message:

1. Open the File menu and choose Mail Document to open the Send Mail/Post News dialog box (see Figure 19.2).

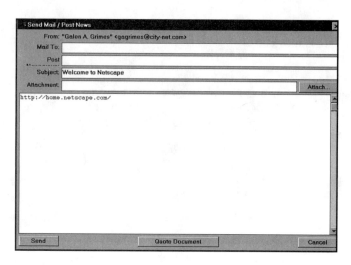

FIGURE 19.2   Send Mail/Post News dialog box.

2. In the **Mail To** field, enter the e-mail address of the person to whom you want to send your message in the form *userid@mail.server*. For example, if you want to send an e-mail message to Netscape (the address is at the bottom of the Netscape home page), type:

info@netscape.com

3. In the **Subject** field, enter an optional subject reference. It's a good idea to enter something in the Subject field to give the recipient an idea of what your e-mail is about before he actually reads it.

4. If you are attaching a file to be sent with the e-mail message, select the Attach button to open the Mail/News Attachments dialog box (see Figure 19.3).

5. If your attachment is part of the document or if it is the document, select the Document radio button, and enter the drive, path, and file name of the file you want to attach. Then indicate whether you want it attached as Document Text, which means it will be the message that is sent, or as Document Source, which means it will be sent as an attached text file.

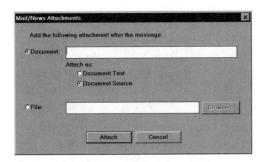

FIGURE 19.3   Mail/News Attachments dialog box.

6. If your attachment is a totally separate file you are sending with the e-mail message, select the File radio button
   and enter the drive, path, and file name. If you are not
   sure of the drive, path, or exact file name, you can select
   the Browse button. This enables you to browse through
   your drives and folders to search for the file (see Figure
   19.4). When you find your file, highlight it and choose
   Open.

FIGURE 19.4   Using Browse to find the file to attach.

7. Finally, select Attach to complete the file attachment and
   return to the Send Mail/Post News dialog box.

8. In the large open text box, enter your message. You can
   type approximately 30K worth of text in the text area.
   You can also include the full text of the current page you
   are viewing by selecting the Quote Document button.

9. Finally, when you have completed your document, select the Send button. This is the electronic equivalent of placing a stamp on a letter and dropping it in a mailbox.

ONE WAY E-MAIL

If you haven't noticed by now, there is one problem with Netscape e-mail. It only works in one direction. You can only send e-mail messages. There's no provision (yet?) for reading incoming messages. Obviously, if you are going to use the Internet for e-mail, you need some way to read the messages (replies) that, sooner or later, you will receive. One solution is to download a shareware e-mail program (Eudora, Pegasus, Email Connection, and so on) from an FTP server. (See Lesson 15 for information on how to access FTP servers.)

One very popular e-mail program is called Eudora. You can download a copy from **ftp://ftp.qualcomm.com**. Go to directory **quest/eudora/windows/1.4** and download the file **eudora144.exe**. You should also download a copy of its manual, **14manual.exe**.

Another up-and-coming e-mail program, E-Mail Connection, can be found at **http://www.connectsoft.com**.

In this lesson, you learned how to use Netscape to send e-mail messages. In the next lesson, you learn how to shop on the Internet.

SHOPPING WITH NETSCAPE

In this lesson, you learn how to use Netscape to shop on the Internet.

SHOPPING THE INTERNET

The Internet was originally designed as a means for transmitting information between university and government sites, but in recent years has expanded to include a variety of additional services. One service area that is still undergoing considerable development on the Internet is the area of commercial development. Businesses are literally scrambling to establish a presence on the Internet and discover its potential for commerce and trade.

Presently, there are numerous shopping outlets available on the Internet. Many give you online catalogs to browse and will take your orders online.

Security Concerns! Despite the assurances of many shopping outlets on the Internet that their transactions are secure, many security experts believe that these transactions are not 100% secure and might still be open to unauthorized accesses. Netscape's attempt to remedy this problem is its secure protocol that can be established between a Netscape Commerce Server and the Netscape browser. When you encounter a Netscape Secure Socket layer protocol connection, you will see the message shown in Figure 20.1 and the broken key shown in the lower-left hand corner will be solid.

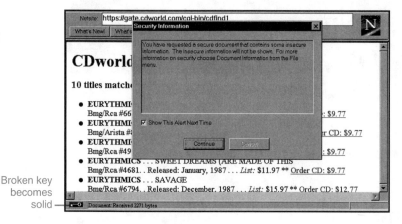

Broken key becomes solid —

FIGURE 20.1   Netscape Secure Commerce Server socket layer security protocol message.

LOCATING ONLINE SHOPPING OUTLETS

One of the best ways to locate shopping outlets on the Internet is to use the Yahoo Web page database (described in Lesson 10) to search on the keyword **shopping**.

While it's impossible to cover even the major shopping outlets available on the Internet, we can give you a sample of some of the companies on the Internet vying for your shopping dollars.

- BookWorld's home page

    http://www.bookworld.com

- Shopping 2000 home page

    http://www.shopping2000.com

- Upper Deck Authenticated collectible sports home page

    http://www.shopping2000.com/ shopping2000/upperdeck

- Venamy Orchids, Inc. home page

  **http://www.shopping2000.com/
  shopping2000/venamy**

- The Ambrosia Catalogue of Fine Wine home page

  **http://www.shopping2000.com/shop-
  ping2000/ambrosia**

- The San Francisco Music Box Company home page

  **http://www.hardiman.com/malls/rmcm/
  musicbox/index.html**

This list of companies is just a small sample of some of the types
of shopping outlets available online on the Internet. If you took
the time to view the home pages listed here, you may have also
noticed that many of the Web pages include 800 numbers. This is
one way many of the companies are handling the still unan-
swered security concerns of having customers post their credit
card numbers online.

Making a Purchase Online

Here's an example of how to make a purchase on the Internet. For
this example, you'll go to CDworld and learn how to purchase a
CD by your favorite artist from the comfort of your living room.

1. Open the File menu and choose Open Location, or click
   the Open button on the toolbar. In the Open Location
   dialog box, type:

   http://gate.cdworld.com/

   to jump to CDworld (see Figure 20.2).

2. Click the CDworld icon (or the Enter CDworld link) to
   jump to the CDworld DISCOUNT Music Store.

Welcome to CDworld DISCOUNT Music Store

offering *over 100,000* CD titles and Music Videos discounted everyday

Now with Netsite Secure Transactions

FIGURE 20.2   CDworld home page.

3. To locate a CD to purchase, click one of the links under **CDs. On Sale**, **Hot Stuff**, or **Featured artists** will give you lists of CDs from which to select. Or you can search for CDs by selecting either the **Select CDs by Artist or Group, Title, or Label** link or the **Select CDs by Music Category** link.

   For this example, select the Select CDs by Artist or Group, Title, or Label link. You'll be prompted to enter search information. Enter enough information to locate the item you want to buy and then press the Search button (see Figure 20.3).

4. If more than one title matches your search query, you will get a list of titles from which to choose. Next to each title is an **Order** link, along with the price of the CD. Links are also provided to allow you to make multiple selections (**Return to Home**) or to check out (**Check Out**).

5. After you make your selection, your order is placed on the Shopping Basket page. Be sure to check that the quantity you want to order is correct. Press the Continue button to preview your purchase and total.

6. Press the Continue button again to provide shipping information (see Figure 20.4), your preferred method of shipping, and your method of payment (see Figure 20.5). Follow the links (by pressing either the Continue or

Continue Order button) to advance to each step. The companies want you to shop here, so they will make the progression of steps very simple and easy to follow.

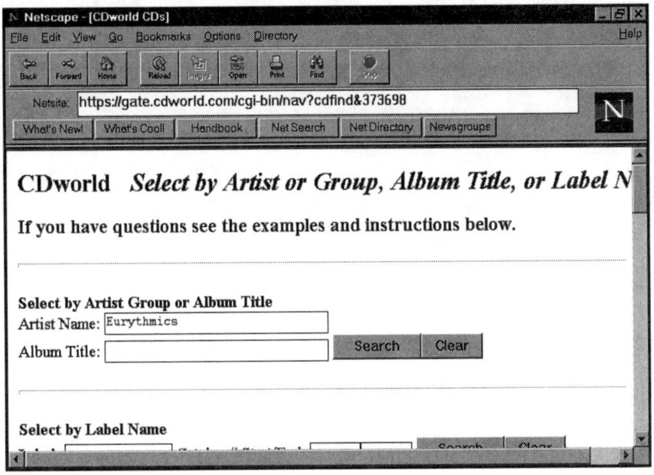

FIGURE 20.3   CDworld search engine.

FIGURE 20.4   Providing shipping info to CDworld.

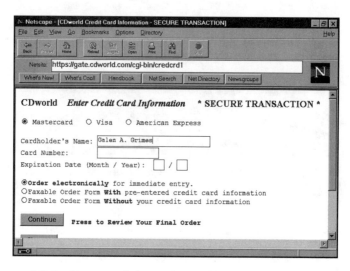

FIGURE 20.5 Payment information to CDworld.

7. Finally, you will be given the chance to review your order before the transaction is completed. If everything looks okay, click the Purchase button to complete the transaction.

As you can see, it's no more difficult than ordering from your favorite catalog. Be aware though that not all online shopping outlets offer "secure" transactions, and not all experts agree on how secure they are.

In this lesson, you learned how to use Netscape to shop online on the Internet. In the next lesson, you learn how to use Netscape to view and save graphic files.

Viewing and Saving Graphic Files

In this lesson, you learn how to view and save various types of graphic files in Netscape.

Netscape and Graphic Files

Netscape does a fairly good job of displaying most of the graphic files you will encounter while browsing the Web. But occasionally, you will run across certain types of graphic files that Netscape is not capable of viewing or displaying. There are dozens of types of graphic files or formats due to the multitude of applications. Multimedia applications have also spawned their share of specialized graphic formats, and more and more Web sites are starting to incorporate multimedia presentations into their Web pages. Lessons 22 and 23 explain some of the multimedia features you may encounter on the Web.

Fortunately, the developers at Netscape realized that trying to design a program that would be a virtual graphics Swiss army knife was impossible, not to mention impractical. So they did the next best thing. They designed Netscape to use what are called *helper applications*.

 Helper Application A helper application for Netscape is one that helps Netscape extend its functionality. Quite simply, it helps Netscape display or use files that it normally would not be able to operate.

GETTING HELPER APPLICATIONS

Before you incorporate a helper application into Netscape, you have to obtain a copy of a helper application program. One helper application program that is extremely useful for viewing additional graphic file formats is called Lview for Windows version 3.1.

There are numerous FTP sites where you can find this program. To save you the trouble of looking, however, the following steps take you to a site that not only provides you with a copy of this program, but is a virtual storehouse of files for numerous types of computers.

1. Open the File menu and choose Open Location, or click the Open button on the toolbar. In the Open Location dialog box, type:

   ftp://gatekeeper.dec.com/pub/micro/ msdos/win31/desktop

Error Trying To Get to FTP Site   If you get an error trying to locate this FTP site, try accessing it minus the directory listing. Try jumping to ftp://gatekeeper.dec.com. Sometimes directory structures change. Remember too, that if the directory structure changes, you may have to look around for the location of the file to download.

2. Look for Lview for Windows in the file **lview31.zip**.

What To Do with ZIP Files   If you don't already have a copy of the file compression utility WinZip, you can get it at this same FTP site. You can find WinZip in the directory **/pub/micro/msdos/win31/util**, in the file **winzip56.exe**. After **winzip56.exe** is downloaded, use the MS-DOS prompt to open a DOS window to run the program (it is actually a compressed file and running it decompresses it into a Windows folder). Read the **README.TXT** file for installation instructions.

3. Use WinZip to decompress **lview31.zip**.

CONFIGURING LVIEW AS A HELPER APPLICATION

Now that you have a copy of Lview for Windows, setting up Netscape to use Lview as a helper application is a snap. This example shows you how to set up Lview to view JPEG (.jpg) files.

Even though Netscape will display JPEG image files on its own without the use of a helper application, using Lview for Windows gives you certain advantages. For example, Lview gives you a variety of options for manipulating the JPEG image file (see Figure 21.1).

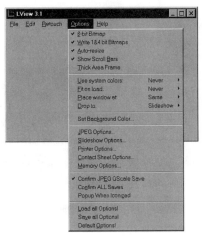

FIGURE 21.1   Lview options.

Lview can also be set up in Netscape as a helper application to view other graphic file formats such as BMP, DIB, and TGA files.

To set up Lview as a helper application:

1. In Netscape, open the Options menu and choose Preferences. Select the Helper Apps tab in the Preferences dialog box.

2. Select image/jpeg as the file type you want to set the helper application to use.

3. In the Action area of the Preferences dialog box, select the Launch Application radio button (see Figure 21.2). Enter the drive and path where lview.exe is stored by choosing the Browse button. Choose OK to save and close the dialog box.

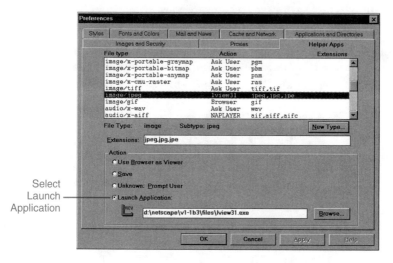

Select Launch Application

FIGURE 21.2 Netscape configured for Lview for Windows.

VIEWING AND SAVING A FILE

To test your newly installed helper application, let's jump to a Web site that has JPEG (.jpg) files you can view using Lview for Windows:

1. Open the File menu and choose Open Location, or click the Open button on the toolbar. In the Open Location dialog box, type **http://clunix.cl.msu.edu/weather/**. This takes you to the page shown in Figure 21.3.

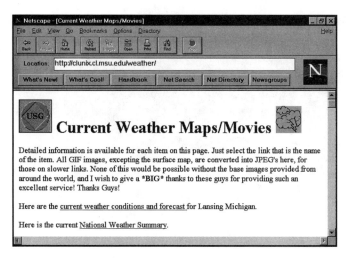

FIGURE 21.3   Current Weather Maps/Movies page.

2. Scroll down the page and select one of the JPEG files linked to this page.

Don't Pick a Large JPEG File!   Don't pick one of the larger JPEG image files—unless you have a fast Internet connection or a lot of time to spare—because it will take a while to download this file before you can view it.

3. After the JPEG image file downloads, Netscape will launch Lview for Windows to display it (see Figure 21.4).

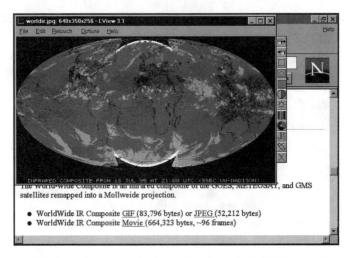

Figure 21.4   Lview for Windows displaying JPEG image file.

In this lesson, you learned how to configure Netscape to use a helper application to view JPEG graphic files. In the next lesson, you learn how to use Netscape to play Web page sounds.

Configuring Netscape To Play Web Page Sound

In this lesson, you learn how to configure Netscape to play Web page sound.

One of the reasons the World Wide Web was created was to bring multimedia to the Internet. While most Web pages are still not living up to that potential, many are. And if you haven't run across a Web page that includes sound, sooner or later, you will. In fact, if you complete this lesson, you will experience sound on the Web.

Getting Sound out of Your PC

Before you can get sound out of the Web, you have to make sure that your PC is equipped to reproduce sound. And it takes more than the tiny (no, make that tinny) speaker that comes with each PC. You will need one of the following:

- A sound card configured to operate under Windows 95 (the sound card vendor supplies the drivers needed to operate in Windows)

- The Windows PC-Speaker driver, a program designed to play Windows audio files on your PC's speaker. You can get a copy from the same FTP site mentioned in Lesson 21, "Viewing and Saving Graphic Files." The file name is **speak.exe** and it's in the **/pub/micro/msdos/win3/sounds** directory.

Driver   A driver is simply a program designed to make a hardware device work and communicate with your PC. Printers, plotters, some hard disks, some modems, and sound cards all use drivers to communicate with your PC.

 It Still Doesn't Sound Crystal Clear!   The PC Speaker driver won't make your PC and its tiny/tinny speaker sound like a symphony. It will just allow you to play certain types of audio files.

Configuring Netscape for Sound

Just as you did in Lesson 21, "Viewing and Saving Graphic Files," when you configured Netscape to use a helper application to display JPEG files, you will need to configure Netscape to use a helper application to play certain types of sound files. One helper application you can use is the Windows 95 Media Player program.

Netscape includes a utility, NPLAYER, that plays some types of audio files. While NPLAYER will play AIF and AU sound files, Media Player will play WAV and MID sound files. Also, Media Player is included with Windows 95.

You will not configure Media Player to play MID sound files in this lesson because they are very rarely used in Web pages. However, if you encounter a Web page that uses them, you should be able to use this lesson as a guide to configure Media Player for MID files.

1. In Netscape, open the Options menu and choose Preferences. In the Preferences dialog box, click the Helper Apps tab (see Figure 22.1).

2. Select audio/x-wav as the **File type** you want the helper application to use.

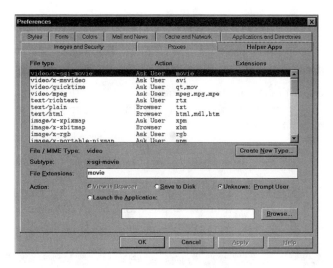

FIGURE 22.1   Netscape's Helper Apps Preferences dialog box.

3. For the **Action** option, select the Launch the Application
   radio button. Enter the drive and path where Media
   Player is stored (see Figure 22.2). (The drive and path
   should be **c:\windows\mplayer.exe** if you did not
   move it.)

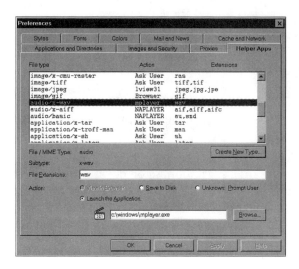

FIGURE 22.2   Netscape configured for Media Player.

DOWNLOADING AND PLAYING SOUNDS

To test your newly installed helper application, let's jump to a Web site that has sound files you can play using Media Player:

1. Open the File menu and choose Open Location, or click the Open button on the toolbar. In the Open Location dialog box, type:

   http://sunsite.unc.edu/pub/multimedia/ pc-sounds/

   This takes you to a Web page where you can test your newly configured helper application. This Web page contains a large sample of WAV files (see Figure 22.3).

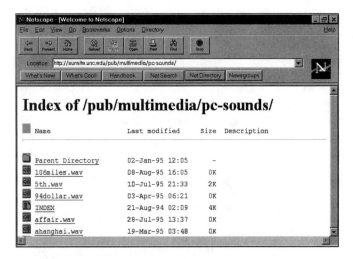

FIGURE 22.3   Location of sample WAV sound files.

2. Select a WAV file to test your newly installed Helper App. If you want a suggestion, scroll down the page a bit and select beback.wav. It's the voice of a fairly well-known actor whom most of you should recognize. Using a 14.4 modem, it should take about 10 seconds to download.

3. When the file is downloaded, Netscape automatically loads the Helper App (see Figure 22.4). Press the first button on the left (the one shaped like a triangle pointing to the right). (When you place the cursor on it, a label appears identifying it as the **Play** button.)

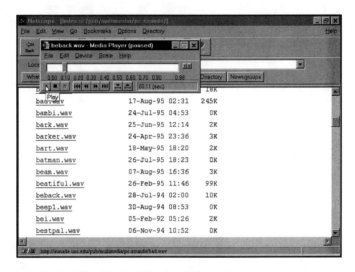

FIGURE 22.4   The Media Player Helper App.

 No Viewer Configured for File Type: audio/basic. Did Not Hear Sound!   This error message indicates that you missed a step or incorrectly configured the helper application. Go back, review the instructions, and try again.

In this lesson, you learned how to configure Netscape to play most types of sound files you will likely encounter on the Internet. In the next lesson, you learn how to configure Netscape for the next extension of multimedia on the Web—full-motion video.

23 CONFIGURING NETSCAPE TO PLAY FULL-MOTION VIDEO

In this lesson, you learn how to configure Netscape to play Web page full-motion video clips.

FULL-MOTION VIDEO

The vast majority of pictures you'll currently find on the Web are static images. Slowly, however, full-motion video clips are emerging as Web authors start to discover new uses for this medium.

 Web Authors   Keep in mind that each Web page you see is a file. These files contain text, graphics, and links to other pages. The person who wrote these pages is often referred to as a Web author.

Full-motion video files tend to be quite large. Before you can view these files, you must download them. The problem that arises with downloading large files is that, depending on the speed of your Internet connection, you may be waiting anywhere from a few seconds (if you're lucky enough to be connected to a T-1 line) to several minutes (if you're using a standard 14.4 bps modem dial-up connection).

 T-1 Line   A T-1 line is the ultimate in high-speed data communications. T-1 lines are capable of moving data at 1.245M per second and are used mainly at corporate and university sites to provide data for Local Area Networks connected to the Internet.

CONFIGURING NETSCAPE FOR FULL-MOTION VIDEO

Fortunately, your PC does not need any special equipment to display most of the full-motion video files you will encounter on the Web. However, Netscape does need another helper application to display full-motion video files—MPEGPLAY.

MPEGPLAY can be found in the compressed file mpegw32g.zip located on **ftp://gatekeeper.dec.com/** in the /pub/micro/ msdos/win3/desktop directory.

Download mpegw32g.zip as you did the other helper applications (described in Lessons 21 and 22) and use WinZip (or PKZIP) to decompress it. MPEGPLAY, however, needs to be installed on your PC before you can configure Netscape to use it. Installation instructions are available in the file README.TXT, which is contained within the compressed file mpegw32g.zip.

After you've installed MPEGPLAY on your PC, you are ready to configure Netscape to use it as a helper application:

1. In Netscape, open the Options menu and choose Preferences. In the Preferences dialog box, select the Helper Apps tab (see Figure 23.1).

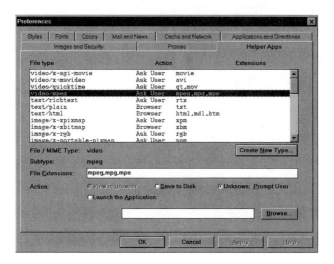

FIGURE 23.1   Netscape's Helper Apps Preferences dialog box.

2. Select video/mpeg as the **File type** you want the helper application to use.

3. For the **Action** option, select the Launch the Application radio button. Enter the drive and path where mpegplay.exe is stored (see Figure 23.2). Click OK.

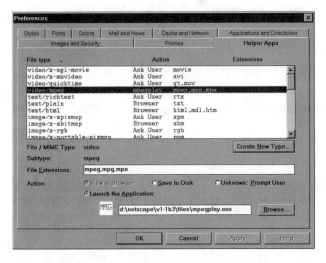

FIGURE 23.2   Netscape configured for MPEGPLAY.

PLAYING FULL-MOTION VIDEO

To test your newly installed helper application, let's jump to a Web site that has MPEG full-motion video files you can play.

1. Open the File menu and choose Open Location, or click the Open button on the toolbar. In the Open Location dialog box, type:

http://clunix.cl.msu.edu/weather/

If this page looks familiar, it's because it's the same page you jumped to in Lesson 21 to view JPEG files by configuring Netscape to use Lview for Windows as a helper application. This time, you will be downloading MPEG full-motion video files to test MPEGPLAY.

2. Scroll down the page until you come to a link labeled **Movie**. These are MPEG full-motion video files. Click the Movie link to begin downloading the file (see Figure 23.3).

FIGURE 23.3   Downloading MPEG full-motion video file.

3. When the file is downloaded, Netscape will launch MPEGPLAY and play the video (see Figure 23.4).

FIGURE 23.4   MPEGPLAY playing a full-motion video.

Oh My Gosh! It's Taking a Long Time To Download This File! Remember, you learned earlier that MPEG files (or, for that matter, full-motion video files in general) tend to be quite large. In the example shown, it took over two minutes to download the video file displayed in Figure 23.4.

In this lesson, you learned how to configure Netscape to use a helper application to play full-motion video files. In the next lesson, you learn how to customize the appearance of Netscape.

CUSTOMIZING NETSCAPE'S APPEARANCE

In this lesson, you learn how to change the way Netscape appears on the screen.

DISPLAYING MORE OF YOUR NETSCAPE SCREEN

If you're viewing Netscape in Windows' standard 640×480 VGA mode, then what you're seeing on your screen could appear a bit cramped. There are, however, a few simple changes you can make to display more on your screen.

REMOVING THE TOOLBAR

The nine icons that make up Netscape's toolbar are simply shortcuts to commands that appear on the File, Edit, View, and Go menus. Removing the toolbar allows you to see more of the current page. To remove the toolbar:

1. Open the Options menu.

2. Choose Show Toolbar to remove the check mark and the toolbar.

REMOVING THE LOCATION FIELD

The Location field displays the URL (Uniform Resource Locators) of the current page. While this information can be quite helpful, it is not essential, and neither is the Location field. If you remove it, you can see even more of your screen:

1. Open the Options menu.

2. Choose Show Location to remove the check mark and the Location field.

Removing the Directory Buttons

The directory buttons on the Netscape screen duplicate commands available to you on the Directory and Help menus. Removing them will allow you to see a bit more of your screen:

1. Open the Options menu.

2. Choose Show Directory Buttons to remove the check mark and the directory buttons.

With the toolbar, Location field, and directory buttons removed, you can now view almost 50% more of the current page (see Figure 24.1).

Figure 24.1   Without the toolbar, Location field, and directory buttons.

Changing Your Video Mode

Another way to display more of the current page on your screen, without removing the toolbar, Location field, and directory buttons, is to change your video mode. If you purchased your PC and monitor within the last three years, there's a good chance they will support a video mode higher than Windows' standard

640×480 VGA mode. Higher resolution video modes are not stan-
dardized, and often go by names like Super VGA, Extended VGA,
and so on; they range in resolution from 800×600 to 1024×768
to 1280×1024. Figures 24.2 and 24.3 show how the screen
changes as you increase the resolution.

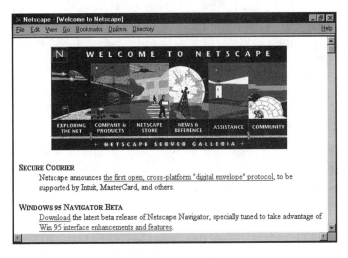

FIGURE 24.2   640×480 Standard VGA.

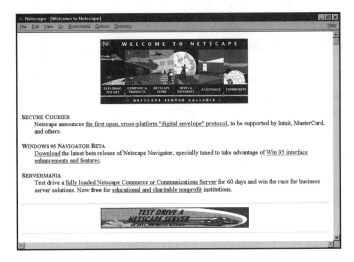

FIGURE 24.3   1024×768 mode.

To change your video resolution:

1. Choose Start on the taskbar to open the Start menu. Then choose Settings, Control Panel.

2. Double-click the Control Panel's Display icon. On the Display Properties sheet, select the Settings tab.

3. Drag the slider in the **Desktop area** to increase or decrease the video resolution. In some cases, Windows will prompt you to restart the operating system to activate the resolution change.

CHANGING COLORS

One thing most users eventually get tired of is seeing the same screen colors day in and day out. Fortunately, if you get bored with Netscape's screen colors, you are given some latitude in setting your own.

To set your own colors:

1. Open the Options menu and choose Preferences.

2. In the Preferences dialog box, select the Colors tab. This displays the Colors Preference screen.

Color choices are purely a matter of taste. If you are so inclined, experiment with different selections. Make sure you select Preferences instead of **Document If Present** or the page you're viewing will set screen colors. Remember, too, to choose OK when you're done.

In this lesson, you learned how to change Netscape's screen appearance. In the next lesson, you learn more ways to configure Netscape.

CONFIGURING NETSCAPE

*In this lesson, you learn how to make
advanced configuration changes in Netscape.*

CHANGING NETSCAPE'S CONFIGURATION OPTIONS

In many cases, Netscape will operate acceptably if you do nothing
that's described in this lesson. But the configuration options described here will help you tailor Netscape to your exact setup. In
some cases, however, if you do not make the proper configuration
settings, there are parts of the Internet you will not be able to
access.

If you are running Netscape on a computer attached to a LAN
(Local Area Network), there's a good chance your systems administrator has already made all of the necessary configuration
changes. If this is how you are running Netscape, make sure you
consult your system administrator before you make any changes
in your configuration.

LAN (Local Area Network) A LAN is merely a group of
computers connected together in order to share certain
resources, such as files, hard disk space, printers, other
external devices, and services. Shared services in the
past were usually limited to application software and
e-mail, but now often include Internet access.

If you are running your copy of Netscape on a stand-alone PC and
you dial in to the Internet using a modem, it's up to you to make
sure you have Netscape configured properly. Running Netscape

stand-alone, as opposed to on a LAN, will also affect some configuration settings. These differences will be explained when you get to them.

All of the configuration settings in this lesson are made in Netscape's Preferences dialog box.

STYLES

The Styles tab (see Figure 25.1) contains options that enable you to set how the toolbar will appear on the screen; whether you start with a blank page, Netscape's home page, or a home page you choose; whether links are underlined; and when links you have visited expire (which means they lose the color change indicating a visit). You can also press the Expire Now button to expire your links at any time.

All of the changes here are cosmetic and have no real effect on how Netscape operates. Feel free to set them according to your personal preferences.

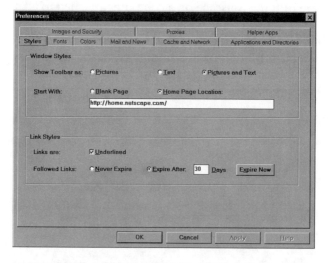

FIGURE 25.1   Style Preferences dialog box.

FONTS

The Fonts tab (see Figure 25.2) has other cosmetic settings concerning the fonts used to display Web pages. Again, you can experiment with these to find settings that suit your personal preferences.

The Encoding options pertain to whether you are using a Latin-based (alphabet) or Japanese-based (character) version of Netscape. Set them according to your personal preferences.

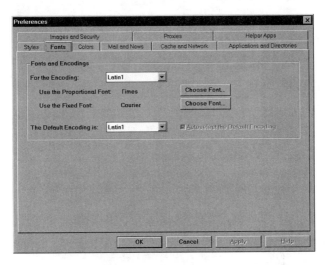

FIGURE 25.2   Fonts Preferences dialog box.

MAIL AND NEWS

Netscape's Mail and News options were covered in Lessons 19 and 17 respectively. Please refer to those lessons for details.

CACHE AND NETWORK

Netscape's Cache and Network Connections settings (see Figure 25.3) were covered and explained in Lesson 4. Please refer to that lesson for details.

The settings for Network Connections only pertain to those operating Netscape on a Local Area Network. You should consult your system administrator before changing either setting.

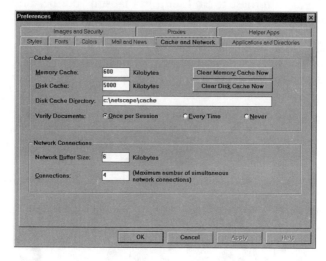

FIGURE 25.3 Cache and Network Preferences.

APPLICATIONS AND DIRECTORIES

The Supporting Applications options (see Figure 25.4) pertain to helper applications you may need to conduct a Telnet session. Here you would list the drive and path of the helper application, an application you might need to assist you in viewing a text-based session, and, if you were conducting the session to an IBM Mainframe, a helper application to control that type of session. If you choose to use the Telnet application supplied with Windows 95, the drive and path will be **c:\windows\telnet.exe**.

The Directories settings determine which directories will be used to store downloaded files and where Netscape will store your bookmark list. You can accept the default settings established when Netscape was installed, or set them to other locations. The Browse button enables you to browse your hard disk for other directories to use.

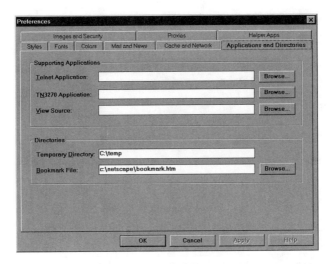

FIGURE 25.4   Applications and Directories Preferences.

IMAGES AND SECURITY

The Images and Security Alerts settings determine how Web page images are displayed on your screen and what action should be taken to alert you to a secure or non-secure Web page.

The Images settings control how Web page image colors are handled and whether Netscape will display partial images while they are loading, or wait until the entire image has been received by your computer before it is displayed. The latter part of this setting is a matter of preference, but the default setting (While Loading) is something that is touted as one of Netscape's advantages over other Web browsers.

PROXIES

If you are running Netscape on a stand-alone PC, the Proxies settings do not pertain to you. They are used when the PC on which you are running Netscape is connected to a Local Area Network, and your system administrator has set up a security system known as a *firewall*.

Firewall?   A firewall is a security measure taken to prevent unauthorized access to a Local Area Network or an Internet server. Like its namesake, firewall, it is a protective barrier that stops movement or access to a given computer system.

The settings made here allow you access through the firewall and will be provided to you by your system administrator.

HELPER APPS

Netscape's Helper Apps settings were covered in Lessons 21, 22, and 23. Please refer to those lessons for details.

In this lesson, you learned how to configure Netscape and set preferences for the options Netscape allows you to control.

Congratulations! You are now an experienced Netscape user. But don't put Que's *10 Minute Guide to Netscape for Windows 95* on the shelf yet. Keep it near your workstation to use as a quick reference whenever you have trouble remembering any of the commands and options covered in these lessons.

How To Download Netscape

In this appendix, you learn how to download Netscape.

Since its initial release, Netscape Navigator has been distributed as shareware from Netscape's FTP server on the Internet.

Shareware Shareware is software that is freely distributed. The author requests that you register the product by sending in the suggested registration fee. Shareware might also be a "limited-use" version of the full product. The version that is distributed "for free" is a sample of the full product; when you register your copy, you are sent a copy of the full version. Netscape distributed as shareware is, however, the full product. A few successful commercial products started out as shareware.

This means that in order to acquire Netscape you have to already have Internet access and a means to download files from an FTP server. Despite this supposed handicap, Netscape has captured an estimated 65-70 percent of the Web browser market.

Windows 95 is the first version of Windows to provide you with access to the Internet (provided you purchased the CD-ROM version or the Microsoft Plus). If you haven't installed Windows 95 Internet access, pull out the instructions and install it. You can then use the FTP program to download Netscape.

If you don't have Windows 95 Internet access or Internet access through another program, you most likely can get one from your Internet Service Provider. If your Internet access is through a Local Area Network connected to the Internet, try your system administrator.

Either way, point your FTP download program to the following URL:

ftp://ftp.netscape.com/pub/netscape/windows/

The URL Is Different!   Depending on whether you download a *beta* or final version, you could wind up downloading out of a different directory than the one shown in this appendix. Beta copies are usually identified in a beta directory (such as /1-?b?/, with the question marks (?) being the version and beta numbers).

For example, the beta version (Netscape 1.2) the author used while writing this book was originally stored in **ftp://ftp.netscape.com/pub/netscape1.2b4**.

Beta   A beta release or beta version of a software product is one that is still under development and may still contain bugs or errors. Beta releases allow you to sample new features the manufacturer is adding to the next commercial release of the program.

If you are running Windows 95 or Windows NT, the file you want is the 32-bit version of Netscape, **n32e11n.exe**. If you are running Windows 3.1 or Windows for Workgroups, the file you want is the 16-bit version, **n16e11n.exe**. Both of these are compressed (archived) files in the ZIP format. They have an EXE file extension instead of a ZIP extension because they are *self-unarchiving* files, which means you do not need a copy of PKUNZIP to unarchive or decompress the files. You merely run this file the same as you would any other EXE file or program.

The developers at Netscape have also gotten into the habit of posting beta copies of Netscape on their FTP server, as well as the current "official" release.

Posting beta copies may be one of the keys to the success of Netscape. Many users simply cannot resist the opportunity to sample a product before it is "officially" released, and despite the fact that Netscape betas are still under development, most have been fairly stable products.

INSTALLING NETSCAPE FOR WINDOWS 95

In this appendix, you learn how to install Netscape for Windows 95.

Installing Netscape under Windows 95 is a snap.

1. Double-click the My Computer icon. Double-click the C: icon (your C: drive).

2. Create a folder (directory) for the file you downloaded from the Netscape FTP server (ftp.netscape.com) by choosing File, New, Folder and entering a name for the new folder. You can simply call it **nettemp**.

3. With both folders open (the folder containing the file and the new one you just created), copy the archive file you downloaded (**n32e11n.exe**) into the new folder by selecting the file and dragging and dropping it to the new folder. Select Copy here.

4. Double-click the file to unarchive the files contained in it.

5. In the Windows 95 Control Panel, double-click the Add/Remove Programs icon.

6. Select the Install button on the Install/Uninstall tab. In the Install Program From Floppy Disk or CD-ROM dialog box, select the Next> button.

7. In the Run Installation Program dialog box, enter the drive and path for the setup program you unarchived in step 4 above. If you're following this example, in the **Command line for installation program** text box, you should enter:

        c:\nettemp\setup.exe

8. Click the Finish> button to begin the installation of Netscape. When prompted, accept the default installation directory (folder), **c:\netscape**, as the location in which to install Netscape.

INSTALLING NETSCAPE FOR WINDOWS 3.1

In this appendix, you learn how to install Netscape for Windows 3.1.

If you're still using Windows 3.1 (or 3.11) or Windows for Workgroups (remember, the author used Windows 95 throughout this book), here's how to install Netscape:

1. Use File Manager to create a new directory for the archive file you downloaded (**n16e11n.exe**) from the Netscape FTP server (ftp.netscape.com). Copy this file into that directory.

2. Double-click n16e11n.exe to unarchive the file.

3. Double-click setup.exe to begin installing Netscape. When prompted, accept the default installation directory, **c:\netscape**, as the directory in which to install Netscape.

INDEX

PLUG YOURSELF INTO...

The Macmillan USA Information SuperLibrary (tm)

See the new SuperLibrary Newsletter

THE MACMILLAN
INFORMATION SUPERLIBRARY™

Free information and vast computer resources from the world's leading computer book publisher—online!

FIND THE BOOKS THAT ARE RIGHT FOR YOU!
A complete online catalog, plus sample chapters and tables of contents!

- **STAY INFORMED** with the latest computer industry news through our online newsletter, press releases, and customized Information SuperLibrary Reports.

- **GET FAST ANSWERS** to your questions about Macmillan Computer Publishing books.

- **VISIT** our online bookstore for the latest information and editions!

- **COMMUNICATE** with our expert authors through e-mail and conferences.

- **DOWNLOAD SOFTWARE** from the immense Macmillan Computer Publishing library:
    - Source code, shareware, freeware, and demos

- **DISCOVER HOT SPOTS** on other parts of the Internet.

- **WIN BOOKS** in ongoing contests and giveaways!

TO PLUG INTO MCP:

WORLD WIDE WEB: http://www.mcp.com

FTP: ftp.mcp.com

Complete and Return this Card
for a *FREE* Computer Book Catalog

Thank you for purchasing this book! You have purchased a superior computer book written expressly for your needs. To continue to provide the kind of up-to-date, pertinent coverage you've come to expect from us, we need to hear from you. Please take a minute to complete and return this self-addressed, postage-paid form. In return, we'll send you a free catalog of all our computer books on topics ranging from word processing to programming and the internet.

Mr. ☐   Mrs. ☐   Ms. ☐   Dr. ☐

Name (first) ☐☐☐☐☐☐☐☐☐☐☐   (M.I.) ☐   (last) ☐☐☐☐☐☐☐☐☐☐☐☐☐☐☐

Address ☐☐☐☐☐☐☐☐☐☐☐☐☐☐☐☐☐☐☐☐☐☐☐☐☐☐☐☐

☐☐☐☐☐☐☐☐☐☐☐☐☐☐☐☐☐☐☐☐☐☐☐☐☐☐☐☐

City ☐☐☐☐☐☐☐☐☐☐☐☐☐☐☐   State ☐☐   Zip ☐☐☐☐☐ ☐☐☐☐

Phone ☐☐☐ ☐☐☐ ☐☐☐☐   Fax ☐☐☐ ☐☐☐ ☐☐☐☐

Company Name ☐☐☐☐☐☐☐☐☐☐☐☐☐☐☐☐☐☐☐☐☐☐☐☐

E-mail address ☐☐☐☐☐☐☐☐☐☐☐☐☐☐☐☐☐☐☐☐☐☐☐☐☐☐☐☐

1. Please check at least (3) influencing factors for purchasing this book.

Front or back cover information on book .... ☐
Special approach to the content .... ☐
Completeness of content .... ☐
Author's reputation .... ☐
Publisher's reputation .... ☐
Book cover design or layout .... ☐
Index or table of contents of book .... ☐
Price of book .... ☐
Special effects, graphics, illustrations .... ☐
Other (Please specify): _____ ☐

2. How did you first learn about this book?

Internet Site .... ☐
Saw in Macmillan Computer
   Publishing catalog .... ☐
Recommended by store personnel .... ☐
Saw the book on bookshelf at store .... ☐
Recommended by a friend .... ☐
Received advertisement in the mail .... ☐
Saw an advertisement in: _____ ☐
Read book review in: _____ ☐
Other (Please specify): _____ ☐

3. How many computer books have you purchased in the last six months?

This book only .... ☐   3 to 5 books .... ☐
2 books .... ☐   More than 5 .... ☐

4. Where did you purchase this book?

Bookstore .... ☐
Computer Store .... ☐
Consumer Electronics Store .... ☐
Department Store .... ☐
Office Club .... ☐
Warehouse Club .... ☐
Mail Order .... ☐
Direct from Publisher .... ☐
Internet site .... ☐
Other (Please specify): .... ☐

5. How long have you been using a computer?

Less than 6 months .. ☐   6 months to a year ..... ☐
1 to 3 years .... ☐   More than 3 years ...... ☐

6. What is your level of experience with personal computers and with the subject of this book?

	With PC's	With subject of book
New	☐	☐
Casual	☐	☐
Accomplished	☐	☐
Expert	☐	☐

Source Code — ISBN: 0-7897-0570-2

7. Which of the following best describes your job title?

Administrative Assistant ☐
Coordinator ☐
Manager/Supervisor ☐
Director ☐
Vice President ☐
President/CEO/COO ☐
Lawyer/Doctor/Medical Professional ☐
Teacher/Educator/Trainer ☐
Engineer/Technician ☐
Consultant ☐
Not employed/Student/Retired ☐
Other (Please specify): ☐

8. Which of the following best describes the area of the company your job title falls under?

Accounting ☐
Engineering ☐
Manufacturing ☐
Marketing ☐
Operations ☐
Sales ☐
Other (Please specify): ☐

9. What is your age?

Under 20 ☐
21-29 ☐
30-39 ☐
40-49 ☐
50-59 ☐
60-over ☐

10. Are you:

Male ☐
Female ☐

11. Which computer publications do you read regularly? (Please list)

_____
_____
_____
_____
_____
_____
_____
_____
_____
_____

Comments: _____
_____
_____

Fold here and scotch-tape to mail.

Il··l··l·l··l·l·ll··ll··l·l·l··l·l··l·l·ll··ll··ll··l··ll··l·l·l